Acting Edition

An Ordinary Muslim

by Hammaad Chaudry

D1535172

ISBN 978-0-573-70941-8

www.concordtheatricals.com
www.concordtheatricals.co.uk

FOR PRODUCTION INQUIRIES

UNITED STATES AND CANADA
info@concordtheatricals.com
1-866-979-0447

UNITED KINGDOM AND EUROPE
licensing@concordtheatricals.co.uk
020-7054-7200

Each title is subject to availability from Concord Theatricals Corp.,
depending upon country of performance. Please be aware that *AN
ORDINARY MUSLIM* may not be licensed by Concord Theatricals
Corp. in your territory. Professional and amateur producers should
contact the nearest Concord Theatricals Corp. office or licensing
partner to verify availability.

This work is published by Samuel French, an imprint of Concord
Theatricals Corp.

MUSIC AND THIRD-PARTY MATERIALS USE NOTE

Licensees are solely responsible for obtaining formal written permission from copyright owners to use copyrighted music and/or other copyrighted third-party materials (e.g., artworks, logos) in the performance of this play and are strongly cautioned to do so. If no such permission is obtained by the licensee, then the licensee must use only original music and materials that the licensee owns and controls. Licensees are solely responsible and liable for clearances of all third-party copyrighted materials, including without limitation music, and shall indemnify the copyright owners of the play(s) and their licensing agent, Concord Theatricals Corp., against any costs, expenses, losses and liabilities arising from the use of such copyrighted third-party materials by licensees. For music, please contact the appropriate music licensing authority in your territory for the rights to any incidental music.

IMPORTANT BILLING AND CREDIT REQUIREMENTS

If you have obtained performance rights to this title, please refer to your licensing agreement for important billing and credit requirements.

AN ORDINARY MUSLIM was first produced by New York Theatre Workshop (James C. Nicola, Artistic Director; Jeremy Blocker, Managing Director) in New York, New York on February 7, 2018. The performance was directed by Jo Bonney, with sets by Neil Patel, costumes by Susan Hilferty, lights by Lap Chi Chu, sound by Elisheba Ittoop, fight direction by Thomas Schall, and dialect coaching by Dawn-Elin Fraser. The production stage manager was Lori Ann Zepp.

AZEEM BHATTI . . . . Sanjit De Silva
SAIMA KHAN . . . . .Purva Bedi
MALIKA BHATTI . . . . Rita Wolf
AKEEL BHATTI . . . . Ranjit Chowdhry
JAVERIA BHATTI-MIRZA . . . . .Angel Desai
DAVID ADKINS . . . . .Andrew Hovelson
HAMZA JAMEEL . . . . Sathya Sridharan
IMRAN JAMEEL . . . . Harsh Nayyar

AN ORDINARY MUSLIM was a recipient of the Edgerton Foundation New Play Award and a Laurents/Hatcher Foundation Theater Development Grant.

CHARACTERS

AZEEM BHATTI – British Pakistani, mid-30s.

SAIMA KHAN – British Pakistani, mid-30s.

MALIKA BHATTI – Pakistani, mid-50s.

AKEEL BHATTI – Pakistani, late 60s.

JAVERIA BHATTI-MIRZA – British Pakistani, late 30s.

DAVID ADKINS – British White, mid- to late 30s.

HAMZA JAMEEL – British Pakistani, mid- to late 20s.

IMRAN JAMEEL – Pakistani, early 70s.

NOTE ON TEXT

A forward slash (/) denotes an overlap in speech.

A dash (–) denotes an interruption.

Ellipsis (…) denotes a trailing off. Within a passage of dialogue (…) denotes a small pause or hesitation.

Asterisk (*) denotes two or more characters talking simultaneously.

Italics and <u>underline</u> denote emphasis.

A glossary is available at the end of the text.

PRODUCTION NOTE

One intermission was taken after Act II, Scene Two for the New York Theatre Workshop production of this play in February 2018.

ACT I

Scene One

(Evening, Friday, September 2011, West London, England. The living room of the Bhatti home. Baby pictures of grandchildren hang on the wall alongside scenic portraits of the English countryside. The living room is decorated with traditional Muslim and South Asian ornaments, a round plate, with the Ayat ul Kursi inscribed hung on the wall, an Adhan clock, a colourful gold inscribed tissue box on the table and so on. **JAVERIA BHATTI-MIRZA**, *dressed in hijab, talks to* **AZEEM BHATTI** *who is offstage in the kitchen.)*

JAVERIA. You're beginning to drive like an old man, you know that right?

AZEEM. You hit menopause yet?

JAVERIA. Takes forty minutes from the station, max, been over an hour.

*(**AZEEM** enters handing a cup of tea to **JAVERIA**.)*

AZEEM. You want me to drive like your boy Saeed?

JAVERIA. Not my –

AZEEM. Still drivin round in his Beema thinkin he's a bad man. Still stinks of curry.

JAVERIA. What you mean "still"? He used to smell alright.

AZEEM. That's because you liked the curry smells you freshy.

JAVERIA. Freshy? Coming from a coconut like you that's a compliment. Where is he now?

AZEEM. Still in Southall.

JAVERIA. He never was that ambitious.

AZEEM. You used to love Southall.

JAVERIA. Still do. As long as you don't have to live there it's great.

AZEEM. You were only able to go thanks to me. Amount of times I had to be your chaperone for your Bollywood films. You owe me, dad would've never let you go on your own.

JAVERIA. I owe you nothing. Only came so you could sneak off to Glassy Junction for a pint.

AZEEM. They've closed it now. (*I'm*) Gutted. Should've been preserved on the National Heritage.

JAVERIA. Are you, gutted?

AZEEM. Course. Felt like doing a janazah prayer for it.

JAVERIA. Seriously befkoof, are you still hittin the Guinness?

AZEEM. Oh...no.

JAVERIA. How long?

AZEEM. Six months.

JAVERIA. Not a drop?

AZEEM. ...Not a drop.

JAVERIA. Masha'Allah that's great, I'm <u>so</u> proud of –

AZEEM. Go away.

JAVERIA. I said Saima would be good for you didn't I?

AZEEM. Yeah, well, I am, I'm gonna take her...

JAVERIA. What?

AZEEM. It's a secret.

JAVERIA. I love secrets!

AZEEM. It's meant to be a surprise.

JAVERIA. I love surprises!

AZEEM. ...takin her to Paris next month. First anniversary 'n all.

JAVERIA. Paris?

AZEEM. Yeah.

JAVERIA. Oh Azeem.

AZEEM. What?

JAVERIA. You're so cliché.

AZEEM. Piss off.

JAVERIA. There are so many places you can –

AZEEM. I have my reasons.

JAVERIA. What are your reasons?

AZEEM. No.

JAVERIA. Tell me... *(Pinches him.)* Tell me!

AZEEM. Ow, stop! Alright... I, er, I want it to be like, to be like *Midnight in Paris*.

JAVERIA. ...The Woody Allen movie?

AZEEM. Yeah. When I saw it, I was like, I would like that. It's nice.

JAVERIA. Sorry. You're not cliché. You're cheesy.

AZEEM. It's not cheesy. It's sweet. Romantic even.

JAVERIA. It's so cheesy Azeem, it's giving me pain just to hear you talk about it.

AZEEM. Piss off. Better than Khalid, buy you a happy meal for your birthday.

JAVERIA. ...Is, is mum upstairs?

AZEEM. He still pissing around in that Prius?

JAVERIA. Is mum okay?

AZEEM. I'd rather ride a bicycle than drive a Prius.

JAVERIA. Did she ask about me?

AZEEM. Why would she ask about you, I'm her favourite.

JAVERIA. ...You're right. Why <u>would</u> she ask about me.

AZEEM. Oh c'mon Baji, she's just spent the whole night in hospital, give her a break will you?

JAVERIA. I just want her to, for once, acknowledge, accept what she –

AZEEM. Can you, for once, just help this family instead of starting a ruckus?

JAVERIA. *I am* helping. I'm taking dad with me aren't I?

AZEEM. You are?

JAVERIA. Yes.

AZEEM. For how long?

JAVERIA. Couple of weeks.

AZEEM. ...Maybe, er, maybe a month?

JAVERIA. Don't push your luck.

> *(Silence.)*

AZEEM. Mum buys gifts, for your kids, in the hope that you'll visit more than once a year. Hoping you'll just drop by sometime. She just collects presents...hoping.

JAVERIA. ...Is her heart actually that bad?

AZEEM. The angina flared up. Cardiologist upped the medication. Could've been a heart attack.

JAVERIA. What reason did she – what excuse did she give to the doctor?

AZEEM. Same shit as when we were younger.

JAVERIA. She fell?

AZEEM. Yep.

JAVERIA. It doesn't make sense though, dad hasn't done anything like this, like, in a lifetime, he's a changed man, were...were you even there last night when it happened?

AZEEM. ...No, why –

JAVERIA. See, so maybe mum started it.

AZEEM. It was dad. Uncle Imran made him feel bad about not being part of his Tablighi Jamaat lot anymore, they wanted him to come for their forty day retreat. I'll give you that, he usually tells them no, keeps his word to mum, but this time, they're doing the chilla in his hometown so –

JAVERIA. Lahore?

AZEEM. Not Pakistan. India. His actual hometown, before Partition.

JAVERIA. Oh, wow, no wonder, dad's never been back there.

AZEEM. So he broke his promise to mum, agreed to go with the Jamaat, and the two of 'em kicked off... Typical Jamaat, causin trouble as always.

JAVERIA. Oh c'mon.

AZEEM. What?

JAVERIA. Azeem, you blame the Jamaat for everything. Deflect responsibility, just like mum. The problem is not the Jamaat, the problem is this family.

AZEEM. Are you seriously making excuses for him right now?

JAVERIA. I'm not! All I'm –

AZEEM. He hit her! After he promised he would never do that shit again.

(*Silence.*)

JAVERIA. He's discovered the Internet.

AZEEM. I know. I'm terrified. Just you wait till I find the guy who introduced him to a computer. Sent me a LinkedIn request the other day.

JAVERIA. Me too, I just accepted.

AZEEM. Why'd you accept it?

JAVERIA. Did you not?

AZEEM. Of course not. I've rejected it three times.

JAVERIA. Why?

AZEEM. First of all, it's a complete lie. He says he's semi-retired when he's been fully retired for three years. Second of all, don't encourage his behavior. Today it's LinkedIn, tomorrow it's Facebook, and then what, Facetime? We have to stop it now.

JAVERIA. His profile pic though, how'd he learn to take a selfie?

AZEEM. Looks like a mug shot. Arrested for crimes against personal hygiene.

JAVERIA. Don't be / mean.

(**SAIMA KHAN** *enters.*)

SAIMA. Baji!

JAVERIA. There she is. You've lost weight.

SAIMA. That's good.

JAVERIA. Not good, too thin as it is…been that stressful living with Azeem?

SAIMA. You don't know the half of it.

JAVERIA. *(Removes her hijab.)* I've said to you so many times, come visit us. Come without this one, I'll have Khalid look after the kids, just us two, it'll be fun.

SAIMA. Hmm, a few days without Azeem, very tempting –

AZEEM. Hey, hey –

SAIMA. He's alright really.

AZEEM. *(Embracing* **SAIMA.***)* Just alright?

SAIMA. *(Playfully nudging* **AZEEM** *away, to* **JAVERIA.***)* ...What's that? *(Noticing the bonnet cap under* **JAVERIA***'s hijab.)* Those look cool, never seen that kind?

JAVERIA. What are you using?

SAIMA. The ones that tie at the back.

JAVERIA. No, use these. They're much better. They're called ninja under scarves, stops your scarf from slipping, ideal if you're on the go, just need to flick your scarf on. I'll send you some. I've been wondering what you look like with it on.

SAIMA. That's right, haven't seen me since I started wearing it have you? This is why you should visit more.

AZEEM. While you're at it, can you show her how to wear it properly as well?

SAIMA. I wear the hijab just fine.

AZEEM. Makes your head look like an egg.

SAIMA. Thanks.

AZEEM. It's like I'm married to humpty dumpty.

JAVERIA. Shut up befkoof.

SAIMA. He's been a right cheeky git since he found out the bank is promoting him to manager, thinks he can get / away with anything.

JAVERIA. Wait, what was that?

AZEEM. *Saima.*

SAIMA. What?

JAVERIA. You're being promoted, to, to manager – that's amazing – why didn't you tell me?

AZEEM. Not meant to tell any – don't want dad to know till things are certain. Concrete.

SAIMA. Thought it was certain.

AZEEM. Just nothing to celebrate about.

JAVERIA. Yet. But soon?

AZEEM. Soon.

JAVERIA. Wow, look at you two, the power couple of West London. *(To* **SAIMA.***)* Azeem told me you're up for a promotion as well?

SAIMA. I'm being considered, but yeah, maybe, hopefully, insha'Allah, just never ends, a client complained today, a shopkeeper, he left out a crate of cans in the sun, then said it was our fault that they were faulty, cheek.

JAVERIA. How did the fundraiser go? Good turnout?

SAIMA. Oh no, I'm still working on that, but it's not really me, it's mainly Hamza who does most of the / organising.

JAVERIA. Oh it's Hamza's who's doing it?

SAIMA. Yeah, he runs the mosque now.

JAVERIA. I haven't seen him in ages. Is he still cute?

SAIMA. I, I don't –

JAVERIA. What I mean is, he's a gentleman...chivalrous.

AZEEM. My arse. Stuff Hamza *and* his old man, took advantage of dad, overcharged him for repair on his car.

JAVERIA. Uncle Imran is so sweet though –

AZEEM. He's a git!

JAVERIA. And Hamza's clearly doing well for –

AZEEM. Are you nuts? He works as a mechanic for his father, ha, he's still back where we were a generation ago. Typical. Quite the poster boy for British Muslims that lad is eh?

SAIMA. He has done some good work for the fundraiser.

AZEEM. Fuck the fundraiser, that's the last thing that should be on your mind right now.

JAVERIA. Why, what's / up?

SAIMA. *(To* **AZEEM.***)* Actually, since you bring it up, I think I'm going to do it now, things have changed.

AZEEM. Everyone in your office convert to Islam?

SAIMA. No.

AZEEM. Then things haven't changed.

JAVERIA. What hasn't changed?

SAIMA. Sheila. She's back.

AZEEM. Who's Sheila and where the hell did she go?

JAVERIA. I have a friend called Sheila.

SAIMA. She's back from maternity leave. Sheila's head of Human Resources. Always has her hair in a bun?

AZEEM. Now that you've narrowed it –

SAIMA. Chatting to her over lunch, told her I had thought about wearing my hijab to work, but then thought again. Sheila said I should do it. I had her full backing, if anyone says anything I should come straight to –

AZEEM. C'mon Saima you're smarter than that.

SAIMA. What?

AZEEM. White people love saying that kind of shit. Makes them feel good about themselves. And then when shit hits the fan, you're the only one who's going be there to pick up the pieces. On your own.

SAIMA. Try it once at least –

AZEEM. Saima, for God's sake, you're being considered for a promotion, you go in wearing your headscarf, you can say goodbye to any –

SAIMA. Could see me outside of work, on the weekend, at the high street, any –

AZEEM. The workplace is a different matter, trust me. You'll compromise your authority – come in with a hijab on your –

SAIMA. I think you're making a bigger deal out of –

JAVERIA. Why have you got such a problem with her / wearing it.

SAIMA. Exactly what I'm saying.

AZEEM. She not tell you about the gora at her work? Something happens on the news, he starts at her "your lot are at it again," "why are your lot causin trouble." Now imagine walking into that same situation, only with a hijab on your head... They'll never accept you.

JAVERIA. Saima, ignore this idiot. I'm not going to bullshit you, if you wear your hijab to your office, suddenly, expect some aggro, every moron will ask you why you wore it, did your husband make you wear it, you'll be seen as the ambassador for Islam. But sod 'em, you don't have to explain who you are to anyone.

AZEEM. Are you stupid? Why are you encouraging her?

JAVERIA. You want to watch how you talk to me?

AZEEM. ...understand this. In this country, a good Muslim is an invisible Muslim. As soon as you become visible, as a Muslim, you're fucked.

JAVERIA. Fine. If that's the case, then, then is it even worth getting a promotion where they're not prepared to accept you as a practicing Muslim.

AZEEM. Is this some sick joke you're trying here?

JAVERIA. What?

AZEEM. You know what.

JAVERIA. No. I don't know what. C'mon, tell me, *what*?

AZEEM. ...Mum and dad depend on both of our incomes. This family needs Saima's...you walked out to leave this family on my shoulders, so now let me take care of it.

JAVERIA. Acha, that's how you feel Azeem?

AZEEM. You're not helping, that's all.

JAVERIA. I'm not – then what the hell am I doing here? Huh? You think taking dad to my home is easy for me? No, it's not. But for you, for mum, for this –

SAIMA. But aunty doesn't want you to...she's forgiven him. She doesn't want him gone.

JAVERIA. Doesn't want him –

SAIMA. *No.

AZEEM. *She does.

SAIMA. Don't lie. Forgiven him, you –

AZEEM. Mum always does this, she doesn't know what's good for her, I know –

JAVERIA. If mum doesn't want him gone, why am I here?

(MALIKA BHATTI *enters the living room from upstairs.*)

MALIKA. Why are you here?

JAVERIA. Asalaam alaikum Mum.

MALIKA. Such care and concern.

JAVERIA. How's your health, your heart, is it all –

MALIKA. Where's Sami?

JAVERIA. Left the kids in Manchester with Khalid.

SAIMA. Aunty, go back upstairs and rest, you should be taking care –

MALIKA. You left my grandson? And you ask me how my heart is. I guess I'll have to wait, what, another one year to see him?

JAVERIA. I just couldn't risk it, that's all. I don't want the children to see their grandparents arguing like this.

MALIKA. Me and your father are fine. But you would have to visit more than once a year to know how your own parents are.

JAVERIA. I'm not here to argue Mum.

MALIKA. Then what are you here for?

AZEEM. Baji's here to –

MALIKA. I'm talking to Javeria.

JAVERIA. Here to make your life easier. To take dad for a few weeks. A month. So you can recover, take some –

MALIKA. My life is fine. I'm fine with your father here. The only thing I wanted from you was to see my grandson, hoping I could spend some time with Sami, but you can't even –

JAVERIA. And Khadijah Mum.

MALIKA. Sami is the youngest. He's the baby –

JAVERIA. And he's the boy. But Khadijah, she, she loves you so much Mum, always talking about her nani, hamaesha laghi rehti hai, "meri nani, meri nani," she even drew you a picture to give –

MALIKA. And I love her. What are you trying to say?

JAVERIA. Nothing.

MALIKA. Did you just come here to accuse me, insult me?

JAVERIA. I, I shouldn't have come. Was a –

MALIKA. Running away now? Go. Go ahead. Run away like you always do.

JAVERIA. Fine, fine. I'm going.

MALIKA. Next time, tell Khalid to come on his own and bring my grandchildren with him. He loves coming here. He loves us. They all love coming here, the children, Khalid, they run to come to London. Only you are the one who runs away from us.

JAVERIA. Not us Mum, <u>you</u>. Run away from you. You didn't leave me any choice but to run away from you.

(*AKEEL BHATTI enters from outside.*)

AKEEL. So much noise, it could only be Javeria.

(*AKEEL hugs her tightly.*)

How are you Beti? Kaisi hai meri Heer? Okay, what's wrong?

JAVERIA. Nothing.

AKEEL. Beti?

JAVERIA. Fine.

AKEEL. Whatever it is, it can't be something ice cream can't fix.

JAVERIA. No Dad –

AKEEL. Mint choc chip, your favourite. Where's Sami and Khadijah? They will enjoy –

JAVERIA. They're not here, I'm –

AKEEL. Why are they not –

JAVERIA. 'Cause I'm here to see you Dad, see if you wanted to come with me.

AKEEL. What do you mean?

JAVERIA. Come stay with me and Khalid for a few weeks. Azeem's packed your suitcase, come with me, have a break from things.

AKEEL. ...Packed my stuff?

JAVERIA. So we can leave now.

AKEEL. Now? You, you're not spending the night.

JAVERIA. No.

AKEEL. You have to spend the – where's Khalid?

JAVERIA. Back home.

AKEEL. *(Deflecting.)* You came without your husband, that's not right, imagine if, if his parents found out – after she gets married, a girl's home is with her husband, you know that, that's how it –

JAVERIA. If you're so fond of him, come see him in person. He'd love to see you.

AKEEL. ...But I got you ice cream.

JAVERIA. We can have some on the way.

AKEEL. It will melt on the way.

JAVERIA. *Dad.*

AKEEL. Are you and Khalid part of the Jamaat?

JAVERIA. Dad, stop changing the subject, once we get –

AKEEL. There's nothing more important than doing tabligh with the Jamaat, that's how I brought you up, you should –

JAVERIA. We're not part of the Jamaat. Our family is all about the Sufi path.

AKEEL. They have Sufi influences.

JAVERIA. Not enough of them...come Dad, what do you say?

(Silence.)

AKEEL. Malika, how's...how's your health?

MALIKA. Fine.

(Pause.)

AKEEL. You, you should be resting. Why don't you lay down? Rest. I was thinking, maybe, maybe once you've recovered, you and Saima, and Javeria Beti, you as well, you all could go out to one of those spas, for the whole day, a girls day out, my treat. What do you think?

MALIKA. I think it's a miracle. In forty years of marriage the most you've ever gotten me is a cup of coffee.

AKEEL. What do you think Saima Beti, won't it be nice to –

SAIMA. I don't know Uncle, I've, I've never been to one, so –

AKEEL. Azeem never sent you? *(To* AZEEM.*)* What kind of husband are you? Then it's done. I'll book it today and –

MALIKA. Akeel...don't book anything.

(Pause.)

AKEEL. I... I met Imran Sahib at the mosque. He, he asked me if I am still committed to going with the Jamaat for forty days to India, complete the chilla with them. I tried explaining, getting out of it. But I gave a commitment, after ten years, I gave them my word, so maybe –

MALIKA. And you gave me your word. No Jamaat for you.

AKEEL. But it's really tough for Pakistanis to get a visa to India.

MALIKA. You gave me your word many years ago. No Jamaat.

AKEEL. Mine has not expired yet, why not take advantage of –

MALIKA. This is not up for discussion Akeel. No Jamaat.

AKEEL. ...If only someone from this family would have carried... Aslam. Aslam's children, his sons, both of Aslam's sons followed him in the Jamaat, the sons followed the example of the father and they kept –

MALIKA. I don't know them.

AZEEM. Yes you do Mum, they used to hang out on the street corner, acting like gangsters. You used to make me cross the road whenever we saw them.

AKEEL. *(Signaling the length of their beards.)* But now they have this big beards, they go with the Jamaat for four months every year.

AZEEM. They used to deal crack. *(To* MALIKA.*)* Drugs.

MALIKA. Good I made you cross the road.

AKEEL. Now they go to prisons, speak to criminals, help reform them, especially the Muslim ones.

AZEEM. That's easy, half of them are their mates.

AKEEL. But Aslam's family, his children, someone from this family should... Saima, Saima Beti, you know Imran and his son Hamza, they lead the Jamaat in our area, they also have a women's Jamaat now at our mosque, you could –

SAIMA. I only help with the fundraiser –

AKEEL. Just talk to them, they're very nice. The Jamaat loaned us the deposit when we first bought this home, this family owes them so much, then, and then they didn't accept a penny in return, karse hasana, forgave the loan, and –

AZEEM. And we were forever in their debt. *(To* **JAVERIA.***)* Sounds like the Mafia.

*(***AZEEM** *and* **JAVERIA** *share a laugh.)*

AKEEL. *(To* **AZEEM.***)* ...Why do you keep making fun of me?

AZEEM. Not making fun of –

AKEEL. Keep insulting me.

JAVERIA. Abba.

AZEEM. Dad. I'm not insulting you, I wouldn't...you don't see how the –

AKEEL. *You* don't see how the Jamaat protected us, you don't know the days of Paki bashing. You, Azeem, are an educated professional. You work in an office. Not on buses or stalls like I did. You haven't had to work three jobs at once. You haven't worked with your hands. You don't know the sacrifices – just know we are where we are today thanks to them, thanks to those –

AZEEM. Where are we Dad? Huh? Where? Before we were hated for the colour of our skin, now we're hated because of the colour of our skin *and* our religion. Great job that. Is that what we call progress?

AKEEL. ...so what Azeem? Has this community failed you? Have I failed you, is that it?

AZEEM. No Dad, you've failed yourself.

SAIMA. *Azeem, that's not right.

JAVERIA. *Stop that. He's still your father, have some respect for God's sake.

AKEEL. Respect Beti? Respect? No one respects me here. In my own home, what I've done for this family, given my –

MALIKA. Akeel, don't play the victim, okay, it doesn't / suit you.

JAVERIA. Leave him alone Mum.

MALIKA. ...I'm talking to my husband.

> *(Pause.)*

JAVERIA. Just come with me... Daddy, please?

> *(Pause.)*

AKEEL. ...Okay Beti.

JAVERIA. Really?

AKEEL. Yes. But you'll stay the night.

JAVERIA. Dad, I –

AKEEL. No, no, you must. It's not right. To just come and go like...one night, at least one night.

JAVERIA. But then you'll leave with me?

AKEEL. ...Yes, yes...let's go see my grandchildren.

JAVERIA. They'll be so happy to see you their nana, we'll have fun, I promise. I'll take a few days off from work, we'll go to some new restaurants I want try out, I'll take care of you Dad.

AKEEL. I know you will Beti.

> *(AKEEL kisses JAVERIA's forehead.)*

Meri Heer.

Scene Two

(Following day, Saturday, early evening. **AZEEM BHATTI** *is opposite* **DAVID ADKINS** *in their local pub,* **DAVID** *drinks a pint,* **AZEEM** *an orange juice. Silence as* **DAVID** *stares at the unwrapped gift in front of him, a garden gnome.)*

AZEEM. It's a garden gnome.

DAVID. I can see that.

(Silence.)

What have I ever done to make you think I would be inclined toward something like this?

AZEEM. C'mon David, I wrapped it an' everything.

DAVID. A pint would've sufficed.

AZEEM. Fine, I'll take it back, still got the receipt, shouldn't have –

DAVID. Alright, alright, don't get pissy – I appreciate it, the gift. Thank you.

AZEEM. ...Welcome.

(Pause.)

And obviously it's...it's er, you know, a thank you, so –

DAVID. Alright you pansy, shut up.

AZEEM. No, but seriously...cheers.

*(***DAVID*** *clinks his glass with* **AZEEM***'s.)*

DAVID. Let's get you a proper drink, hardly a celebration with –

AZEEM. I'm alright.

DAVID. Eh?

AZEEM. I'm alright.

DAVID. ...Religious reasons?

AZEEM. Yeah.

DAVID. Piss off.

AZEEM. Serious.

DAVID. Since when?

AZEEM. Been trying for a while – it's a process, not like a light switch, takes time.

DAVID. Is this why we keep meeting at Starbucks?

AZEEM. Yeah.

> *(Silence.)*

DAVID. Well...fuck me mate...this is boring.

AZEEM. Didn't realise I was here to entertain you.

> *(Pause.)*

DAVID. I mean, good for you, I guess – *I* can still drink can't I? Or is that –

AZEEM. Yes you can still drink you infidel.

DAVID. ...in that case, good for you an' all that...tell you what is a shame, be on my tod for lunch now.

AZEEM. C'mon now David, I'm sure you and your new mate Richard can –

DAVID. We're not that –

AZEEM. You go to lunch with him more than me, even went to Wembley with him, watched an American football / game together.

DAVID. You said you hated American football, called it a poor man's rugby.

AZEEM. Would've went for the atmosphere –

DAVID. Called them pussies for wearing helmets, shoulder –

AZEEM. The experience, / live sport.

DAVID. You're impossible.

AZEEM. Didn't even ask / me.

DAVID. You said you didn't like...

>   *(Silence.)*

>   In a month, they're doing a U.K. tour, got tickets, we'll go to that.

AZEEM. Already got tickets?

DAVID. Yeah.

AZEEM. Next month?

DAVID. Yeah.

AZEEM. Just you and me?

DAVID. Yes.

AZEEM. ...I don't really like American football.

DAVID. Go fuck yourself.

>   *(Silence.)*

AZEEM. One thing that'll be / nice is –

DAVID. Shut up, done talking to you, go choke on your halal orange juice.

AZEEM. Fine, forget it, it was daft anyway...

DAVID. ...what?

AZEEM. ...The nameplate. Yeah, becoming manager at Clapham, triffic, better pay, more holidays, all good stuff...but, the dream, the dream was the engraved door nameplate, my own nameplate. Like what you see in the films.

DAVID. Right, yeah. Like *Ally McBeal.*

AZEEM. Yeah – no not like *Ally McBeal* you twat. That's not even a movie it's a television show.

DAVID. Banter mate. Know what you mean, course I... I get it.

(*Pause.*)

AZEEM. Azeem Bhatti, dash, manager. Wait, no. Azeem Bhatti, colon, manager.

DAVID. Don't be silly... Azeem Bhatti, underline, and beneath that in capitals, manager.

AZEEM. That's...see, that's why I bought you the garden gnome.

DAVID. Lucky me eh?

AZEEM. ...I mean it though, you stuck your neck out for me, went over Richard, put my name in, this promotion it, it...

DAVID. Means a lot.

AZEEM. Means everything...once it's set in stone then you and I can properly celebrate. Nearly there – still need to get that written reference, make it official, so...

DAVID. So? Richard will give you that.

(*Silence.*)

Saw Saima the other day, coming out of her mosque, she / mention it?

AZEEM. It's not her mosque.

DAVID. What?

AZEEM. You said you saw Saima at "her" mosque, but it's not her – it's *a* – she just helps with the fundraiser there, raising money for the Pakistan earthquake – I mean, Pakistan doesn't get much help, people don't think of it as exotic, not somewhere you go for a honeymoon or a gap year, so sod 'em right? They're a breeding ground for terrorists anyway. So someone has to help.

DAVID. ...I'm glad we cleared that up.

AZEEM. But she knows, I tell her, should also work for people here in London, for British charities as –

DAVID. I think Saima's doing great, especially since her husband does fuck all.

AZEEM. You're not Fidel Castro yourself pal.

DAVID. I at least still campaign for The Labour Party here and there, but you...after a few anti-war marches you just gave up.

AZEEM. Didn't give up mate. Got real.

DAVID. Ever the pessimist.

AZEEM. Well did we stop the war on Iraq David? Did we? Tell me my friend, how many wars have we stopped?

DAVID. Don't know about you but I've stopped a couple.

(*Pause.*)

AZEEM. I can't sort it with Richard.

(*Silence.*)

I can't make peace with Richard. I can't ask him.

DAVID. What, er, what are you going to do then?

AZEEM. It doesn't have to be *his* reference. A reference from this branch is, from someone senior. Say, someone like the second in command...

(**DAVID** *laughs.*)

DAVID. (*Stops laughing.*) Oh, you're serious...well, while you're at it, why not take a kidney as well?

AZEEM. It's a lot, I / realise that.

DAVID. He's still my boss. You forget that?

AZEEM. You're mates though.

DAVID. Oh c'mon, this is business. He's already going to be pissed I went behind his back to help you get this gig and – I can get in serious shit for what you're asking, there could be disciplinary / action.

AZEEM. David, look. Please. Don't make me go to a racist and ask for his help.

DAVID. Racist? He's not...is, is Islam even a race? Does that count?

AZEEM. Fine. He's not a racist. He's a bigot. Is that better? You seen how he is with me.

DAVID. I, er, I've seen how you two are with each other.

AZEEM. Come again?

DAVID. I, I'm just...like last week, right, that. Ten year anniversary of nine eleven, Richard holds a nice little one minute silence in the office and you...you just happen to choose that moment to go for a piss.

AZEEM. ...I had three cartons of Ribena.

DAVID. See.

AZEEM. You reckon for the ten year anniversary of the Iraq war, he'll hold a one minute silence then?

DAVID. That doesn't –

AZEEM. Actually, remind me, when we were marching against the Iraq war, what side was Richard on?

DAVID. So he's a Conservative. Doesn't make him a racist.

AZEEM. Doesn't it?

DAVID. Asking Richard for a reference isn't groveling to a racist. Alright? It's a / basic formality.

AZEEM. At our annual barbecue, he kicked up such a fuss because I asked for some of the meat to be halal.

DAVID. Well, some of these halal butchers, the way they slaughter the animal it's – it was the welfare aspect he was concerned about, you can understand that.

AZEEM. On your lunch break, you two came back with McDonald's...what did you two order?

DAVID. He, er, he had a Big Mac.

AZEEM. Hmm.

DAVID. *I* ordered a McFlurry...and a McChicken Sandwich.

AZEEM. But halal meat turns you into an animal rights activist?

DAVID. Not *me*, I'm not the – all I'm trying to say is that Richard's not what – I mean he dated a Bengali lady.

AZEEM. Oh c'mon, are you –

DAVID. She was darker than you.

AZEEM. Course she was, she was Bengali. But exactly, dated her for a while, fucked her, that's all, the white man conquering the brown woman...like Pocahontas all over again.

DAVID. His mate from uni, shit it's er, Raj! Yeah, you met him, Raj, Asian bloke.

AZEEM. Fella who supports the England cricket team? Not Asian in my book.

DAVID. That's unfair, what, you don't support England as your second team?

AZEEM. Why should I support England when England doesn't support me?

DAVID. Christ Azeem, don't do – look... *(Small pause.)* "tolerance is the prerogative of humanity."

(Pause.)

That's, that's Voltaire.

AZEEM. Oh, it's that wanker.

DAVID. I mean, it's The Enlightenment.

AZEEM. ...

DAVID. What I'm saying is, this is who we are, and we should –

AZEEM. "We"?

DAVID. ...We.

(*Pause.*)

For fuck's sake I'm taking your side – I'm saying that you're not wrong, tolerance is who we are and Richard could, and, and should be more tolerant of your way of life.

AZEEM. I don't want to be tolerated. I want to be respected.

(*Silence.*)

DAVID. There was a time when you and Richard were friends.

AZEEM. Not friends, friendly. When he thought I was a secular Muslim. When he saw me sneak out for Friday prayers, saw that Allah and Islam stuff mattered to me, he was not so friendly anymore.

DAVID. You hide it pretty well, people assume you're just an ordinary Muslim not / someone who –

AZEEM. The type of Muslim you lot could stomach?

DAVID. I didn't mean –

AZEEM. I don't have a lot of friends, but for the few I do, I'd take a bullet.

DAVID. And I, I would take some shrapnel...

AZEEM. ...I wonder...

DAVID. What?

AZEEM. Back in the days of Bush. Blair. Afghanistan, Iraq. You wouldn't have blinked.

DAVID. Why are you taking it there?

AZEEM. Back then, would you have even been mates with someone like Richard?

(Silence.)

DAVID. You're asking a lot, I can't –

AZEEM. This thing with Richard, it's not unique. I've had it before. It's everywhere you go in this country. But let me tell you this. I didn't choose this fight. But, my friend, I can't lose it like my dad and his generation did. Because unlike them, this country is it for me. You get me? Mate, I can barely speak Urdu, English is the only language I know. This, here, this country is all I know, this is all I have...

(Pause.)

I can't go to Richard.

DAVID. ...Right...

AZEEM. So who do I go to?

(Pause.)

DAVID. ...You go to your mate. I will write the reference.

AZEEM. Yeah?

DAVID. Yes...but let me tell you something, get ready to kick your wifey out, because if I get the sack, I'm shacking up with you.

AZEEM. Mate, you do this for me, I'll even let you be the little spoon.

Scene Three

(That night, living room of the Bhatti home.)

AZEEM. Go get them will you?

SAIMA. They're coming down.

AZEEM. Why is *she* taking so long? We'll miss the train. I mean, dad has shit to pack, Baji's got nothing, only stayed one night, frickin diva, likes, likes to keep people waiting, that's all.

> *(Pause.)*

I can't have him stay in this home, not after what he did.

SAIMA. Okay.

> *(Pause.)*

AZEEM. ...This, er, this happened all the time when I was younger and I couldn't do anything about it. I couldn't protect mum, even if I tried I got smacked down.

SAIMA. I didn't know –

AZEEM. See, dad stopped the abuse when mum's heart problem started, after her surgery, he made a promise, he would be a new man, leave his old friends, mum even stopped the Jamaat from coming to this home –

SAIMA. Didn't realize it / was that –

AZEEM. And, and for ten years he's been fine and...he broke that promise. He has to go.

SAIMA. ...That's horrible, I'm so sorry you had –

AZEEM. I don't want your pity.

SAIMA. *Azeem*, I'm not –

AZEEM. He can't stay. You understand? He has to go, I have no choice.

SAIMA. I do. I understand...he has to go.

> *(Pause.)*

...Azeem...you are a good son. You're not doing anything wrong. I support you.

> *(Silence as **SAIMA** comforts him.)*

AZEEM. ...I got some news earlier today. From David.

SAIMA. ...about your job?

AZEEM. Your husband's a manager.

SAIMA. *Azeem*...that's amazing. I knew you'd do it. I said, didn't I? Didn't I?

AZEEM. Yeah, you said.

SAIMA. See, *you're* amazing.

> *(They kiss. **AKEEL** enters with his suitcase forcing **AZEEM** and **SAIMA** to pull back.)*

AKEEL. Saima Beti, will you tell Javeria I'm ready to leave.

SAIMA. Yes Uncle, of course.

> *(**SAIMA** exits upstairs.)*

AZEEM. *(Reaching for **AKEEL**'s suitcase.)* Here, I'll put it in the boot.

AKEEL. Leave it. I can carry it myself. Easily. Our generation grew up on buffalo milk, we have village strength.

AZEEM. Congratulations.

> *(Pause. **AKEEL** leaves for the main exit.)*

...Dad.

AKEEL. What?

AZEEM. I... I got the promotion.

(Pause.)

AKEEL. ...what promotion?

AZEEM. The bank is promoting me to the manager's position. At, at another branch in Clapham. By the time you come back, I'll be –

AKEEL. Promoted?

> *(Silence.* **AKEEL** *interrupts the silence with laughter.)*

A, a promotion. In my lifetime, I never, never...in forty years of work, <u>forty years</u> of work I never once got a promotion, they never liked promoting Pakistanis, I knew it, but I campaigned, complained to the union, nothing, nothing and you...well...

> *(Pause.)*

Mr. Manager.

> *(Silence.)*

AZEEM. So you don't have to worry about money, finances, or any sort –

AKEEL. Wear a tie. On your first day as manager. Make sure you wear a tie. I see young people wearing suits without ties, it's not right.

AZEEM. Alright, I'll wear a tie.

AKEEL. Your grandfather always wore a tie. Sign of a respectable man. Very respected he was, our whole family was, you should know, you should, we're not less than anyone.

AZEEM. I know, I know, heard it all –

AKEEL. Our family, in India, we were landlords, we had wealth –

AZEEM. Landlords?

AKEEL. Yes.

AZEEM. *Owned* the land?

AKEEL. Yes! We had wealth, status, but then Partition. Partition happened. They took our land away from us, and in Pakistan we were like peasants. It all changed... They don't like promoting Pakistanis here.

AZEEM. You, er, never mentioned we were landlords.

AKEEL. Sometimes it's better to forget.

> (**SAIMA** *enters.*)

SAIMA. Baji's coming down.

> (**AZEEM** *takes the suitcase.*)

AKEEL. I said I can / take it.

AZEEM. Save your village strength.

> (**AZEEM** *exits through the main entrance.*)

> (*Silence.*)

AKEEL. Waiting for Javeria, story of my life, I tell you, since she was a little girl... I spoilt her is what I did... When the ice cream van came, and you know the music, how it goes, "ding dong, ding dong," her mother would close all the windows, so Javeria couldn't hear...but Javeria heard. Javeria always heard. I would get every penny together, every time I made sure she got her ice cream. I did right by her.

> (*Pause.*)

I did right by this family, penny by penny... I did right Beti...

> (*Silence.*)

I worry sometimes.

SAIMA. About?

AKEEL. You.

SAIMA. What about me?

AKEEL. That you might be too good for us.

(**SAIMA** *laughs.* **AZEEM** *reenters.*)

SAIMA. Maybe just Azeem.

AZEEM. What?

AKEEL. (*To* **AZEEM.**) Nothing... (*To* **SAIMA.**) and yes.

(**JAVERIA** *enters from upstairs.*)

Maybe just Azeem what?

JAVERIA. Ready?

AZEEM. Waitin on you your highness.

(**MALIKA** *enters with a bag in hand.*)

AKEEL. So...we, we leave...

JAVERIA. Asalaam alaikum Mum.

MALIKA. ...I have gifts. Nothing much, few toys, clothes.

JAVERIA. ...The kids will love that...thank you.

(**JAVERIA** *takes the bag from* **MALIKA** *and looks inside.*)

I'll bring them to visit soon insha'Allah, I promise, maybe they can come on their...

(*Pause.*)

Mum...what is this?

MALIKA. Gifts.

JAVERIA. These are all for Sami, where are Khadijah's... where are your granddaughter's gifts?

MALIKA. She's too old for a gift.

JAVERIA. She's *four*. You always do this, birthdays, Eid, any –

MALIKA. Sami is the baby of the family.

JAVERIA. Don't lie, that's not why.

MALIKA. Watch how you talk to me. Seems like you've lost the little respect / you had for me.

JAVERIA. I come here, leave my family for you, come take dad –

MALIKA. You haven't done anything for me. Did I say I wanted you to take your father? But you still went against me and –

JAVERIA. Well maybe he needed to go then.

MALIKA. Am I that difficult to live with?

JAVERIA. Yeah you are!

AZEEM. Baji doesn't mean it, she's –

MALIKA. Do you have something to say Javeria?

AZEEM. She's not trying to –

MALIKA. *(To* **AZEEM.***)* Be quiet. *(To* **JAVERIA.***)* You have something to say, then say it.

JAVERIA. Nothing.

MALIKA. Because there is nothing. Nothing. Before you start shouting / at me –

JAVERIA. How can you say that? How – you can't seriously – you can't mean that, there's nothing...*nothing*?

MALIKA. Nothing.

AKEEL. Beti, let's leave this, it's not –

JAVERIA. You've always complained about the way dad was with you, with Azeem, but what about the way you were with me? What about the beatings you gave me, the abuse you gave –

MALIKA. Abuse? What're you talking – nonsense. It, it wasn't – okay, a few times, I had to discipline you, sometimes I had to –

JAVERIA. "Had" to? What the hell does that –

MALIKA. You, you, it wasn't – you were badly behaved, someone had to punish you, or –

JAVERIA. Punish? You would beat me for no reason, you –

MALIKA. I, that's only because, because –

JAVERIA. Because what?

MALIKA. You don't know what I got from your father.

AKEEL. C'mon now –

JAVERIA. So you gave that to me? Admit it, you hated me. You hated that you gave birth to a girl and not a boy, that is –

MALIKA. I hated myself! I –

JAVERIA. Oh please enough of your –

MALIKA. Your father made me hate / myself, hate being a woman –

JAVERIA. No more excuses!

MALIKA. I was protecting you!

JAVERIA. What? What were you –

MALIKA. Someone had to punish you, if not me then, then – / I was –

AKEEL. Malika enough!

MALIKA. What?

AKEEL. I'm leaving aren't I? Is that not enough?

AZEEM. Baji let's just / leave.

MALIKA. Is that some favour you are / doing us?

JAVERIA. Let's just go Dad.

AKEEL. Malika, not my daughter. Don't go there.

MALIKA. I want her to know if it wasn't for you I, I would not have been the way I –

AKEEL. Rubbish Malika, you're just blaming me so...

MALIKA. So what?

AKEEL. Beti let's leave this here.

(As AKEEL *leaves,* MALIKA *pulls him back.)*

Don't put your hands / on me.

MALIKA. Say what you were going to say, so what?

AKEEL. You're blaming me so you don't have to accept that you are a failed mother. There, I said it. You could never be a proper mother to your own daughter.

MALIKA. Akeel Bhatti, you are a coward. If it wasn't for you, there would be no abuse in this home, this would be a happy / home.

AKEEL. Rubbish – daffa hoja.

*(*MALIKA *blocks* AKEEL's *path and pushes him back.)*

I said don't raise your / hands to me.

MALIKA. I want to hear you admit it / that you were the cause of this.

AZEEM. Mum please don't, just / let him go.

AKEEL. A woman like you deserves to be divorced.

*(*MALIKA *pushes* AKEEL *again.)*

MALIKA. Tell my daughter you created / this mess.

AKEEL. How can you call yourself somebody's wife.

JAVERIA. Dad come with me.

AKEEL. Let this be the last we see of / each other.

MALIKA. Not till you speak the truth. *Admit what you did, say it's your fault –

JAVERIA. *Both of you please stop this right –

>   (MALIKA *pushes* AKEEL *again and* AKEEL *hits* MALIKA *dropping her to the ground.*)

AZEEM. *(Frozen on the spot.)* Dad.

JAVERIA. *(Comforting* MALIKA.*)* Mum...

MALIKA. *(Slowly rising to her feet.)* ...I'm fine.

>   *(Silence.)*

AKEEL. ...She was, she was pushing – you saw, you saw, she raised her hands to me first, I didn't do – I did right by you Javeria, I did, I did right – Saima Beti, this is not who I am, I am not – she raised her hands first, you saw, you all – I, I raised this family, I worked, penny by penny, I built this home, I sacrificed, I, I did right, I did, I'm a good man... I'm a good man!

ACT II

Scene One

(Forty days have passed. The living room of the Bhatti home, **SAIMA** *is dressed in a trouser suit, hijab with briefcase by her side.)*

SAIMA. You just getting in now?

AZEEM. Had to work late.

SAIMA. My manager husband…that word, "manager," can't believe it…

AZEEM. Why, you thought I couldn't do it?

SAIMA. …Azeem, I'm the one who *always* thought you could do it.

>   *(Pause.)*

I'm really proud of you Azeem.

>   *(***SAIMA*** *holds* **AZEEM** *tightly and kisses him.* **AZEEM** *nudges her away.)*

AZEEM. Not that dad's in the house now.

>   *(Takes her jacket and hijab off.)*

SAIMA. Well, how about the forty days dad wasn't in the house?

AZEEM. C'mon now it's only been – it has not been forty days.

SAIMA. I'm like Moses in the desert.

AZEEM. Stop it will you.

(*Pause.*)

Where is he?

SAIMA. Upstairs, sleeping.

AZEEM. What's, what's he like?

SAIMA. What do you mean what's he – I haven't met uncle yet, I mean, he only came back this morning.

AZEEM. Dad always used to come back worse from the Jamaat. Self-righteous.

SAIMA. *You* sent him on Jamaat for forty days so you / can't exactly –

AZEEM. What choice did I have? Baji wouldn't take him with her would she? Had to send him somewhere after what he did.

SAIMA. Right, okay, I know, I –

AZEEM. No you don't know.

SAIMA. Don't be like that with me.

AZEEM. Like what?

SAIMA. Snappy, pissy. You've been like this for weeks now, *before* uncle came back. I, I get it. Since my promotion, I've been stressed too. The workload drastically increases, more responsibility, and other pressures, but I don't take it out on you, so can you please show me the same respect?

AZEEM. ...What did your boss say?

SAIMA. Are you even listening / to me?

AZEEM. Did you ask your boss for a transfer?

SAIMA. ...Yes, I asked him for a transfer to another office.

(*Pause.*)

He said it's costly to train somebody new for my position, and especially since they just gave me a promotion, they don't –

AZEEM. He said no? Can, can he even – did, did you not tell them you're getting subtle bigotry at work?

SAIMA. Not even subtle any – yes, I did. Told him it's gotten worse since I started wearing hijab to work, people just come – told him about Keith cracking jokes about me fasting, throwing food in my face and being –

AZEEM. And?

SAIMA. And my boss said he thought fasting was a load of bollocks.

AZEEM. Your boss said you fasting was a –

SAIMA. But I said to him, said, that when it's Lent, people fast from –

AZEEM. Yes, and?

SAIMA. ...He said Christianity was a load of bollocks as well.

AZEEM. These fucking gorey, they never fail –

SAIMA. Don't get worked up, I actually think it's for the best.

AZEEM. How?

SAIMA. You're manager.

AZEEM. Okay.

SAIMA. I mean, I can leave my job. I don't have put up with their crap anymore. Put on a scarf, becomes open season, but alhamdulillah, now I can just walk out... I was thinking, some time off, then I can look for a new position. I'm free!

(Pause.)

...Azeem?

AZEEM. What, what you going to do in between, I mean, time off, what, what does that mean?

SAIMA. It means relax! For once in my life, since school I've always had a job, even through university I worked on the / weekend.

AZEEM. What, you just gonna be at home?

SAIMA. I'll do things of –

AZEEM. You just want to be a traditional housewife now? Never had you down as the type.

SAIMA. Why are you being – isn't this the kind of stuff you've had to deal with?

AZEEM. Which is why I told you not to wear the hijab to work.

(Silence.)

I don't think you leaving your job is… I'm saying no, no guarantee, another job is hard to come by… Sheila. Your mate. Head of human resources has her hair in a bun Sheila. Get her to sort / it out.

SAIMA. Don't want to involve Sheila in this.

AZEEM. It's her job.

SAIMA. She's…she's already been doing her job, for me.

AZEEM. …Saima? … *Saima.*

SAIMA. So… I asked for an official prayer space to pray namaz at work.

AZEEM. Are you, are you fucking kidding me?

SAIMA. What? I can't keep combining zuhr and asr, it's rukhsa, and by the time I get home nowadays it's already maghrib.

AZEEM. What, what am / I married to?

SAIMA. Before you say anything, it's not just me, another person. Claire. Convert. Or revert. But Muslim. Nobody knew. Young white girl from the counties. She kept it quiet, hidden, but once she saw me wearing the hijab in the office, she came out with it, so there.

AZEEM. ...You want a prayer space in their building *and* you took one of their people. They must be shitting bricks you're gonna build a minaret on their roof next.

SAIMA. Look, I can't go to Sheila, she's been working very hard to get me that prayer –

AZEEM. Not much point if you're leaving is it?

SAIMA. Yes, of course it is, for sisters like Claire.

AZEEM. Sisters? That's sweet. Wonder where the fuck these sisters and brothers are when shit hits the fan like this. If the ummah is a body then we must be the back side eh Saima?

SAIMA. What is happening / to you?

AZEEM. Tired of this shit. Even our anniversary...

SAIMA. What?

AZEEM. Ruined it.

SAIMA. I, I ruined / it?

AZEEM. Wanted *Midnight in Paris* got nightmare in Paris.

SAIMA. They shout abuse at me and it's my fault?

AZEEM. If you dress like an Algerian asylum seeker then yes.

(*Silence.*)

Go to Sheila, get her to sort it out.

SAIMA. It's not fair on –

AZEEM. Then take your scarf off.

SAIMA. ...how, how can you say that / to me?

AZEEM. At least when you go to work, at your office. Don't put this family at...stay at your job.

(**MALIKA** *enters with* **AKEEL.**)

AKEEL. Asalaam alaikum wa rahmatullahi wa barakatuhu.

SAIMA. ...Wa alaikum salaam.

AZEEM. Salaam.

AKEEL. ...Saima Beti, congratulations on your promotion.

SAIMA. Aw, thank you Uncle. How, how was the Jamaat, how was India? You take any pictures?

AKEEL. I tried, but didn't work, this phone of mine, it's too complicated. But we were mostly in the mosques. Not much sightseeing. It's tough there, the mosques, they stink from the toilets, no proper sewage system. The Muslims there are treated so badly...but I did get to see my old home, the one before Partition, that used to belong to our family.

SAIMA. Oh wow, did, did you go inside?

AKEEL. I did, yes, didn't think I would be able to, but it was a good Hindu family, they let me in. I saw everything. The house has changed, but the fields, the land, the land is still the same...so much land...we should be millionaires today, we should.

MALIKA. Saima Beti, go make some chai for your uncle.

(**SAIMA** *exits into the kitchen.*)

AKEEL. Malika, I say to hell with the British, let's move back home to Pakistan.

MALIKA. Okay.

AKEEL. Okay, yes?

MALIKA. Okay as in I've heard this all before.

AKEEL. You don't understand. In India, speaking your own language, wearing your own clothes, breathing your own air, your land is your land. Everyone looks like you, dresses like you, talks like you, you don't have to explain things always, you can just be...

(**AZEEM** *leaves for upstairs.*)

MALIKA. Azeem, stay –

AZEEM. I'm tired. Start early tomorrow.

MALIKA. Spend some time –

AZEEM. Some other –

(**SAIMA** *enters.*)

SAIMA. Azeem, are you –

AZEEM. What?

SAIMA. Are you taking the car tomorrow?

AZEEM. It's my car, so yes, I'm taking it.

SAIMA. I need it in the evening.

AZEEM. Why?

SAIMA. Working at the mosque, so –

AZEEM. Why're you still working there? The fundraiser's done.

SAIMA. Was asked to participate in the women's committee, have an input into the running –

AZEEM. You want to keep working there then make your own way, not my –

SAIMA. Could you not at least give me a –

AZEEM. Are you deaf? I said I –

AKEEL. Speak to your wife with respect.

(*Pause.*)

You will pick her up.

AZEEM. ...Fine.

> (**SAIMA** *exits into the kitchen.*)

AKEEL. (*As* **AZEEM** *exits upstairs.*) Azeem.

AZEEM. Yes.

AKEEL. ...You wore a tie, didn't you?

AZEEM. What?

AKEEL. Your first day as manager, you wore a tie?

AZEEM. ...Yes Dad, I wore a tie.

> (**AZEEM** *exits. Silence.*)

AKEEL. ...Azeem...talking like that to his wife, it's not right, not right to talk like that.

MALIKA. I wonder where he gets it from.

AKEEL. ...You er, think, you think...is that what *he* thinks?

> (*Silence.*)

How's, how's your health Malika?

MALIKA. Alhamdulillah, it's good. These past forty days, gave me a lot of time to rest. The doctor was happy. He also said I should make sure it stays that way...

> (**AKEEL** *looks around to make sure no one is there.*)

...I can walk to the end of the road all by myself. I climb the stairs twice a day, before I could only –

AKEEL. Malika.

MALIKA. What?

AKEEL. (*Taking out a necklace from his pocket.*) I, I got you this necklace... I sneaked out to the market and got it for you. Kaisa, kaisa laga...?

> (**MALIKA** *does not take the necklace from*
> **AKEEL.** *He places it down on the table.*
> *Silence.*)

...I er, out...outside my home, in Pakistan, there was
this street lamp.

MALIKA. Yes, they have them in London too.

AKEEL. Not like this. I would sit under that light to study,
to read...to be educated. That light was my life, that
light brought us here... I... I came from nothing Malika.

> (*Long silence.* **AKEEL** *speaks in Urdu.*)

Mein maanta hoon,	*I do accept*
Maanta hoon,	*do accept*
Mein...mein ek toota hua insaan hoon.	*I...I am a broken human*
Lekin akhir insaan to hoon.	*But I am after all human.*
Ma bap jawaani mein marga.	*Mother, father passed away in my youth*
Milee barde bhaion ki maar.	*Received elder brothers' abuse*
Pyaar tho door ki baat.	*Love was a distant thing*
Mohabbat kiya hoti hai...?	*What is love...?*
...Jo mila, wo diya.	*...What I got, I gave.*
Ab kabar ke kareeb akar asaas hota hai apni galti ka.	*Now with closeness to the grave, comes a realizing of my mistake.*
Bachpan mein tootgya tha.	*In youth I was broken*
...Toota hua adhmi hoon mein.	*...I am a broken man.*

> (*Silence.* **MALIKA** *picks up the necklace and
> observes it.*)

MALIKA. Acha hai.

AKEEL. What?

MALIKA. It's a nice necklace Akeel.

AKEEL. It...it is?

MALIKA. ...Yes.

> (**MALIKA** *wears the necklace.*)

AKEEL. ...Beautiful.

MALIKA. Yes, I said, it's a nice necklace.

AKEEL. Not the necklace...not the necklace.

Scene Two

*(Next day, evening. **AZEEM** and **DAVID** return to the pub, opposite each other, both are drinking a pint of lager each.)*

DAVID. ...Have to admit, nothing quite hits the spot like a pint... Good to have you back on the dark side.

(Awkward laugh. Pause.)

Let's get you another pint.

AZEEM. What did Clapham say?

DAVID. I wish, I wish you had listened to me. Didn't hand your notice in, resign, and just walk out like –

AZEEM. I couldn't take Richard anymore, so I had no –

DAVID. But I said to you, I said...where are you working now?

AZEEM. Woking.

DAVID. Woking? Fuck, that's far. Why not London? What're you doing in Woking?

AZEEM. Stay on / topic.

DAVID. But is it a good place though? Can you keep working / there.

AZEEM. No. Definitely not. But why would I? I'm going to be the manager of the Clapham branch.

(Pause.)

When do I start David?

DAVID. ...You don't –

AZEEM. Don't say that. Don't you dare – you said you gave the reference –

DAVID. I did! And it was glowing.

AZEEM. ...Richard. I know it. He said –

DAVID. Not Richard, he didn't do –

AZEEM. Don't defend your mate, I know –

DAVID. It wasn't Richard, it wasn't the reference. It was you.

> *(Pause.)*

It was a simple meet 'n greet Azeem. You had it. You had the manager's position, so why go in acting like you were the CEO? Asking for more pay, more holidays – baffles me – asking for things that no manager at any other branch has, surely, you knew that you...

AZEEM. You weren't there, you don't –

> *(Silence.)*

DAVID. You at least owe me an explanation at the very –

AZEEM. I owe you?

DAVID. ...Did they take you to a shit restaurant? A hole in the wall? What got you so –

AZEEM. They, they took me to The Ritz.

DAVID. Oh well, the tragedy.

AZEEM. ...We sat down. I arrived a few minutes late, but no problem. All good. Having a good chat. Life 'n stuff. They asked my what kind of wine I wanted.

DAVID. Here we go.

AZEEM. I said I don't drink wine.

DAVID. Hmm.

AZEEM. Or any alcoholoic beverage. Because I'm –

DAVID. Muslim.

AZEEM. Muslim.

DAVID. So what they do? Pour it down your throat?

AZEEM. They were very understanding, and even said "good for you"...they asked me what mosque I go to, told them I don't really have a mosque.

DAVID. Okay.

AZEEM. Then one of the fella's talks about the extremist mosque near his home in North London. Where Muslims keep having their anti-Britain rallies.

DAVID. ...What'd you say?

AZEEM. I joked, *joked*, "You know my people, we can never say 'no' to a good riot." ...and they laughed.

DAVID. ...You told a joke and they laughed.

AZEEM. It was a different kind of laugh. The, the wrong kind of laugh, they, they weren't laughing <u>with</u> me...it was a laugh that said "See, I knew it, those savages."

DAVID. ...Alright, so they laughed a –

AZEEM. No, it's not them, it's me. That laugh showed, in that moment, I had made myself the House Muslim... I was their token Paki... I've, I've never hated myself so much...

(*Silence.*)

Go back to them. Get them to meet me again. A proper –

DAVID. They've filled the post. The Clapham branch has their manager.

AZEEM. I... I told my...

(*Pause.*)

DAVID. Look, it's not all – if you're earning decent money, I mean, enough to stay afloat, then you –

AZEEM. I work as a waiter. In Woking. I dress in a waistcoat, bowtie and serve drunk white people curries. I'm a waiter.

DAVID. ...Are, are you kidding me...?

(**AZEEM** *shakes his head to say "no."*)

Mate, what're you doin to yourself?

AZEEM. I need you to get me that –

DAVID. No, I need you to listen to me. Help me save you from yourself. Spoke to Richard. Connected with him, on a human level and –

AZEEM. Richard's human? Could'a fooled –

DAVID. Shut up and listen will you. I got through to him. He's struggling to fill your old post, so made him see sense, why hire someone new for projects that you've already worked on, have experience with, save time, money, with you...so he said if you were willing to sort things out, he would consider the possibility of having you back.

AZEEM. What does that mean, sort things out?

DAVID. ...if you were willing to apologise to Richard for past remarks, for the upsetness caused, undermining him, then he'd be willing to put it all in the past. And a, a gentleman's agreement, for best behaviour in the future.

(*Silence.* **AZEEM** *breaks out in laughter.*)

AZEEM. I'm not going back and groveling to a racist, bigot... This isn't just about me dickhead, it's much bigger than me, it's about –

DAVID. It is bigger than you. It's about *you* needing to understand people like Richard. You can't keep fighting the world and calling anyone who doesn't chime in with you a racist. I don't agree with everything Richard says, but – understand this, this country, it's changing. The culture is changing. Now, granted, I accept that better than someone like Richard does, but it doesn't look like the country our parents grew up in, or in fact, even doesn't look like the country *we* grew up in. The streets are different, the clothes are – not saying that's a bad thing. It's not. But that scares some people. You don't have to agree with that fear, but you should respect it, respect that fear. It won't stay this – go back to Richard, make amends, sort your life out – but things will get better, easier, with time, people such as yourself 'n your family start integrating more, then there'll be –

AZEEM. Start integrating? Fucking integrating? I didn't get off the boat yesterday. I'm already integrated. As is my wife, my sister, we were born here. My sister now has children who're born here. This country isn't changing, it already <u>has</u> changed. Some people need to catch up with that fact. I'm as much part of this country and this culture as any fucker here. So let's stop talking about Richard and these poor little white pussies who get "scared," and let's start talking about <u>me</u>. Who I am and what I'm about. Let's start talking about people in this country getting used to to my way of living. And it better happen fast. Because people like me are not going anywhere, we're here to stay... This beautiful brown Muslim face you see in front of you, <u>this</u> is the face of Britain now.

DAVID. I'm not – you're talkin to me as if I'm the one – makin me out to be as bad as Richard when obviously I'm on your –

AZEEM. Maybe you're worse.

DAVID. What? How the hell am I –

AZEEM. Why not? 'Cause you don't call me a Paki or a nigger? Setting the bar a bit low for yourself aren't you pal?

DAVID. I was there on those anti-war marches alongside you, don't forget that.

AZEEM. Easy to be against something that's happening over there and do fuck all about what's happening back here in your own home.

DAVID. Fuck you Azeem. If it makes it easier for you to paint me out to be some – but I've been actively against those things more than even you have, I've always been against anyone bombing anyone, against killing of any kind, us doing it to Muslims or...

AZEEM. ...Or...?

DAVID. ...Or Muslims killing us here.

AZEEM. Is that right David?

DAVID. It's not wrong. At the end of the day, it wasn't upset Iraqis that blew themselves up here in London. It was British born Pakistani Muslims. These people, mate, they had fucking Yorkshire accents. These people were born here. Not just here, look around, elsewhere, Europe, America, anywhere, it's not Iraqis or even Afghanis seeking revenge, it's, it's Muslims born or brought up in those countries, who've lived in those countries, who have the passports of those countries, who speak the language of those countries, they're doing the killing, not...acknowledging that doesn't make me a bigot, or a racist –

AZEEM. No, no it doesn't.

DAVID. No.

AZEEM. Doesn't make you much of a friend either.

DAVID. Not a friend? Then what the hell has all of this been for? Why am I risking my livelihood to help you out, get you a job, something –

AZEEM. I don't want a job. I want dignity. Can you give me that mate? 'Cause you've done a great job of takin it away from me.

DAVID. What on earth have I done to take your dignity?

AZEEM. What've you done? What have you – you colonised my country for two hundred years, you –

DAVID. Ha! Me? *I* did all –

AZEEM. Yes, *you.*

DAVID. Yeah / yeah –

AZEEM. Yeah, yeah, yeah. You. Richard. Your parents. Their parents. Your whole fucking lot. You robbed my land killing anyone who got in the way, doing it all to make your own country richer. What, David, you never wondered how Great Britain became "great"? Then you fuckers promised my dad riches if he came and rebuilt your country after your "secular" World Wars, and you never once, not once, gave him a promotion. After all that, you <u>still</u> keep killing us, bombing Muslims any chance you get... So David, is it any wonder that people such as those British Muslims, with their British passports, have finally woken up and decided to start killing you back?

DAVID. Stop.

AZEEM. Truth is, when I see a Muslim go after you fuckers, however big or small it may bc... I get it. It's hard not to.

(Pause.)

AZEEM. ...I don't have a history, I don't have a heritage, I... I don't even know who I am. And I hate you so much for that.

DAVID. Alright, alright... Things have gotten a bit out of – actually, I shouldn't – at the end of the day mate, you and I, we, we're on –

AZEEM. There is no "we."

DAVID. Yes there is. You and me Azeem, we're mates and we're on the same side, okay? / Granted, things got a little –

AZEEM. Nah. We're not on the same side. Don't think we have been for a while mate. But maybe, maybe we'll get lucky. Maybe America will start another war bombing Muslims, then liberals will like my people again, take to the streets, and we'll all be marching together, holding hands, singing Kumbaya. But till then, we're not on the same side. So I have to make sure my side wins.

Scene Three

(Same day, night. The main prayer room of the local mosque. The mosque is a ground floor flat converted into a mosque. The main prayer room consists of green carpet. HAMZA JAMEEL takes a small bottle of ithar and applies some on himself. He is set to begin prayer when a slightly soaked SAIMA enters.)

HAMZA. You're still here?

SAIMA. Well done Hamza. You're a quick one aren't...sorry. I'm pissed because it's pissin outside and Azeem still isn't here. He was going to pick me up after meeting David, and his damn phone is off – why the fuck does he always have to be –

HAMZA. Saima, mosque.

SAIMA. ...Astaghfirullah.

HAMZA. Typical.

SAIMA. Thought you prayed isha already?

HAMZA. Adding the nafl prayer.

SAIMA. Ahhh Hamza, make me feel terrible, haven't done any nafl since like last Ramadan.

HAMZA. ...Sorry?

SAIMA. Don't be sorry you idiot. It's my fault.

HAMZA. I agree, it is your fault. You should pray your nafl.

SAIMA. Don't make / me feel –

HAMZA. I'm joking, it's...you've got a lot on your plate Saima, so / makes sense.

SAIMA. You don't even...

HAMZA. ...I don't even...?

SAIMA. ...Thought about leaving my job.

HAMZA. Gotten that bad?

SAIMA. Pretty / much.

HAMZA. I'm sorry, I feel terrible –

SAIMA. You have nothing to be sorry –

HAMZA. I feel like I egged you on or / something.

SAIMA. Can you please stop. You're the only one who supported me, thank God for you, I...there's nothing more freeing than being yourself publicly, not having to hide it, I should be thanking you.

(*Silence.*)

I...honestly, between you and me, I thought I could deal with it, take it on... Guess I'm not as strong as I thought I was.

HAMZA. I'm truly sorry to hear that.

SAIMA. Scheduled an appointment with Human Resources, going to speak to my mate Sheila, see if she can...just...

HAMZA. Just?

SAIMA. Just don't want to work there anymore, or anywhere, I'm just, I'm done. You know?

HAMZA. Yes, I know. Course I know, it's the story of every other person in our community. A brother had to leave his job 'cause he refused to trim his beard. In fact, just recently, speaking to a sister who lost her teaching position for wearing niqab.

SAIMA. So what, what do you think –

HAMZA. What do *you* want to do?

SAIMA. I... I want to leave it all. Just not work for a while.

HAMZA. I'm sure all that hassle has taken a toll on you. Taken it out of you.

SAIMA. Exactly!

HAMZA. You must be exhausted Saima.

SAIMA. I am.

HAMZA. I don't know how you've coped this long. I couldn't.

SAIMA. ...A break. Rest.

HAMZA. Then do that. Rest. You owe it to yourself.

SAIMA. No, I can't –

HAMZA. Why not?

SAIMA. It's important I keep my – I'll speak to H.R. –

HAMZA. More important than your well-being? God's placed your mind, your heart as a trust to you, you have to take care of it. You have to take care of yourself.

(Pause.)

SAIMA. Thanks.

(Silence.)

HAMZA. Can I make a suggestion?

SAIMA. Please.

HAMZA. The Jamaat is leaving for a three day ijtimah to Leeds later this month. Getting detached from the dunya, a three day break could be just the cure for you.

SAIMA. ...Maybe some other time.

HAMZA. Why?

SAIMA. No, I –

HAMZA. You get on well with everyone here don't –

SAIMA. I do, I know, only, Azeem isn't that –

HAMZA. Ah, of course, brother Azeem. Have to say Saima, didn't have you down as the obedient housewife?

SAIMA. Stop.

HAMZA. Joking. But you get on with Aisha don't you?

SAIMA. Yeah we're good mates, we even –

HAMZA. She's the one who'll be leading the sisters' Jamaat. You'll be with the sisters for three days, men and women are separate. So don't be worried about seeing my ugly mug all the time.

SAIMA. Don't be silly, it's not that, it'll be –

HAMZA. It's not?

SAIMA. No.

HAMZA. I don't have an ugly mug?

> *(Pause.)*

SAIMA. Azeem's probably still hanging out with David, better I call a cab, or try for / the bus.

HAMZA. Been getting a lot of marriage proposals from Pakistan recently...

SAIMA. I'm sure you're spoilt for choice, after all, you have so many cousins to choose from.

HAMZA. Oh okay, is that how it is?

SAIMA. Yes.

HAMZA. ...Speaking about cousins, I do have a cousin in Woking. You ever been?

SAIMA. No.

HAMZA. Oh you must. Tell Azeem to take you for a day trip, maybe even meet my cousin, he knows about everything that goes on there.

SAIMA. Why, what goes on there?

HAMZA. ...Nothing.

SAIMA. What were you / going to –

HAMZA. Nothing, nothing, just trying to...trying to wind you up. Pissing around, being daft...sorry.

(**AZEEM** *enters.*)

AZEEM. Been honkin the horn for ages, pissin outside, make me come in –

HAMZA. Asalaam alaikum brother Azeem, we were just talking about you.

AZEEM. (*To* **SAIMA.**) Shall we go?

HAMZA. Brother, don't leave just yet. Been years since I've seen you in this masjid.

AZEEM. There are other masjids than –

HAMZA. Oh I wasn't implying –

AZEEM. Course not.

SAIMA. Come.

HAMZA. I think you would really enjoy your time here now. I've changed a lot of things.

AZEEM. Don't doubt it for a second.

HAMZA. The new tafseer classes seem to go down well. Everybody loves the fundraising events we have, charity runs, that kind of stuff. Which must be why everybody pitches in, gets involved.

AZEEM. Sounds terrific. Later mate.

HAMZA. Might make sense to you now why Saima likes it here so much. Would be nice to have her husband also take an interest.

AZEEM. ...Yeah? Go on. Tell me more about this revolution that you're leading here Hamza?

HAMZA. I didn't say / I was leading –

AZEEM. Tell me something important that is different. 'Cause I can smell the piss from the hole in the ground toilets from here. So what's new?

HAMZA. I was merely suggesting that perhaps come for jumah, here, sometime. The khutbah is in English now, more students have now started –

AZEEM. Wow, English? That *is* a big step for your lot. *(In a mocking Pakistani accent.)* A for Apple, B for Ball, C for Cat –

SAIMA. Let's go, we're not getting / anywhere here.

HAMZA. Yeah go Azeem, listen to your wife.

AZEEM. You got something to say, / say it.

HAMZA. Saying it aren't I – always havin pop at us, I hear from people what you say, bad mouthing the Jamaat, having a go at this community, no reason for it. You just need somebody to blame. But the Jamaat has done a lot of good in our –

AZEEM. Oh do me a favour mate. Doing good? You and your village Islam lot are the reason Muslims are on their knees in this country. Have you even taken a look at yourself? You look like the fucking Taliban. Your beards don't have to be that long mate, wearing shalwar kameez, fuck you wearin that for? Wear a suit, look presentable – and then, then, you start praying in the street, in front of everyone, in the middle of the fucking day. I mean, no wonder these gorey hate us, you're shoving it down their fucking throat.

HAMZA. Please don't swear inside the mosque.

AZEEM. Ha, what a joke. That's all you have to / say is it.

HAMZA. Oh no, I get it.

AZEEM. You do, do you?

HAMZA. Yeah mate, I get it. I see it. See what the problem is. It's a big problem...insecure Muslims. Major problem this ummah has today.

SAIMA. *Stop it now Hamza.

AZEEM. *Hear this cunt?

HAMZA. My brother, all I'm saying is you are ummah'ti Muhammad, be proud of that. Have a bit more self-confidence. Be a confident Muslim, not an insecure one.

SAIMA. I said stop it, leave / it alone.

HAMZA. Maybe, maybe I'm wrong. Take your approach. Maybe we should all just hide away as Muslims, go hide in some corner and do as we're told. And, and just in case they confuse us for radicals, we should shave off our beards as well. Would that work for you Azeem? Why not eh? After all, you already got us takin off the hijabs, so I guess our beards –

AZEEM. Hijab?

HAMZA. ...I one hundred per cent support Saima's decision to wear her headscarf to her work place, or wherever she would like.

AZEEM. Don't talk about my wife like you know her. You don't know her.

HAMZA. But am I wrong though? Not wrong / am I?

AZEEM. Yes you're wrong.

SAIMA. *(To* **AZEEM.***)* I'm leaving, and you should / come with me.

AZEEM. You're so wrong I don't even know where to –

SAIMA. Please just let it be Azeem! For once in your life let something go.

AZEEM. *(To* **SAIMA.***)* Can I not talk now? Why can't I talk? Can you just let me talk? *(To* **HAMZA.***)* Radical?

That coming from you non-political pacifist lot. The problem is not that you're "radical." No, no, no. The problem is that you're not radical enough. Every gora in this country should know that if they lay a finger on a Muslim their next stop will be the cemetery, then see if some whiteboy rips off somebody's hijab. You're right, let's be self-confident Muslims. After all, Britain belongs to us. If they're not ready to give us what everybody else has, then we have to be ready to take it, *as a community*, my "dear brother." I don't want you to hide away in some corner. Oh no. Not. At. All. I want the opposite. I want to give them a reason to fucking fear us.

SAIMA. ...You've gone from no Islam to Nation of Islam in five seconds.

AZEEM. You what?

SAIMA. ...Joke, was a –

AZEEM. Since when was I no Islam? Huh? How the fuck am I no Islam exactly? 'Cause I'm not as self-righteous as you or the son of a preacher man over here? 'Cause I don't have the outfit, do the lingo and the special handshake?

SAIMA. No, I didn't mean – don't get – sorry, okay. I didn't mean –

AZEEM. Like fuck you didn't. Too Muslim for some, not Muslim enough for others. Story of my life. I pay the price for being Muslim, so don't you dare try –

HAMZA. Don't speak like that to her.

AZEEM. ...Haha, sorry, er, come again?

HAMZA. The best of Muslims are the ones who are best to their wives.

AZEEM. Aww. That's / cute isn't it?

SAIMA. Stop, stop, please.

(Embracing **AZEEM** *and lightly pulling him toward the exit.)*

Listen to me. Please. Azeem, look at me – I didn't mean it, wasn't thinking when talking, let's go. Leave this. I don't like seeing...

AZEEM. ...what?

SAIMA. Come closer a –

AZEEM. No.

SAIMA. Let me smell your breath.

(Pause.)

You didn't...? You wouldn't, wouldn't do that to us... please, tell me you didn't?

(Silence.)

AZEEM. Can, can we talk...let's go home.

(**SAIMA** *approaches* **AZEEM,** *puts her hand in his trouser pocket and takes the keys to the car.)*

SAIMA. Salaam Hamza.

AZEEM. Can you at least hear me –

SAIMA. Maybe I'll let you know about Leeds after all.

(**SAIMA** *exits.)*

HAMZA. Oh yeaaah...forgot about that. Old habits die hard I guess. Should've let me know bruv, would'a had a fry up ready / for you.

AZEEM. What's in Leeds?

HAMZA. Bro, bro, bro, don't involve me in your domestic. I'm just the son of a preacher man innit.

(Pause.)

...Aite man, come. Call you a cab.

AZEEM. I can sort it.

HAMZA. Course you can.

> (*As* **AZEEM** *is leaving.*)

Mate...

AZEEM. What?

> (*Pause.*)

HAMZA. What happened...? To you, I mean. Back in school, you were the class clown, and now, now you're –

AZEEM. You were in my school?

HAMZA. You takin the piss?

> (*Pause.*)

You seriously don't...yes Azeem. I was a few years below you, but we all used to play footy together at lunch. We even played on the same team sometimes...mind the time Rizwan was about to save my shot 'n you pulled his trousers down...it's how all the lads found out he wasn't circumcised... Had us all in fits you did. Like always.

> (**AZEEM** *shakes his head to say "no."*)

Honestly, you...you don't remember that...the footy?

> (*Pause.*)

...the laughs?

AZEEM. No.

Scene Four

(Next day. Evening. The living room of the Bhatti home. MALIKA is lying down on the sofa with her head on SAIMA's lap. SAIMA is threading MALIKA's eyebrows.)

SAIMA. It's okay Aunty, makes sense, uncle's back, you have to look your bestest –

MALIKA. Not for him, I –

SAIMA. Don't worry Aunty, I won't tell.

MALIKA. Forget your Uncle, if you shaved my eyebrows he still wouldn't notice.

(They laugh together.)

SAIMA. It's good you and uncle are going for a meal. Nice. Why don't we ever go? It's been so long. Actually, they're showing Bollywood films at the cinema again, how about I get us tickets and book a restaurant beforehand.

MALIKA. Forget Bollywood, the films are all so violent.

SAIMA. No, it's Shah Rukh Khan, all romance.

MALIKA. ...Book a ticket for Azeem as well.

SAIMA. Just us two will be nice.

MALIKA. Ask him at least?

SAIMA. Azeem doesn't like Shah Rukh Khan.

MALIKA. Why?

SAIMA. Probably jealous of him I guess.

MALIKA. Nothing to be jealous of. Azeem's much more handsome than Shah Rukh Khan.

SAIMA. Yes, yes of course. Azeem's the most handsome boy in the world.

MALIKA. ...You two were arguing all last night.

    (Pause.)

Poor boy slept on the sofa.

SAIMA. He's lucky it wasn't the shed.

MALIKA. Kya hua Beti? ...Bolo?

    (Silence.)

SAIMA. ...Aunty?

MALIKA. Ji Beti?

SAIMA. How would you feel...would you mind...if I went with the Jamaat, for the ijtimah, a weekend, just three days.

MALIKA. ...Jamaat?

SAIMA. I know, you have issues with them, because of uncle, makes sense, and I, I'm not joining them or anything, they won't come to the house, not even the women. A one off, not going to be a part –

MALIKA. Then why?

SAIMA. A breather.

MALIKA. Be like normal people, go to hotel in Italy, a resort, anywhere in Europe –

SAIMA. I'm just, stretched, so busy, missing my salah, going away somewhere where I can focus on prayer, reading Qur'an, not being constantly distracted by worldly life, would be nice. The opportunity's there, so why –

MALIKA. What opportunity?

SAIMA. There's an ijtimah in Leeds coming up. There's a group leaving from –

MALIKA. How do you know?

SAIMA. Hamza told me.

MALIKA. Is he going?

SAIMA. He always goes. Reminds me, I should pray nafl with Aisha tonight. Hamza's pretty good about that. And he's a big Shah Rukh Khan fan, go figure.

MALIKA. Are you going there tonight?

SAIMA. Yes, after this.

MALIKA. How much longer will you keep working at the mosque? The fundraiser's done.

SAIMA. I don't really "work" there, just sometime – why?

MALIKA. Why do you think?

SAIMA. Aunty...c'mon. It's not like that. In this day and age, girls and guys are friends, it's very common.

MALIKA. Beti, we watched *Harry Met Sally* together.

SAIMA. *(Laughs.)* You're funny.

MALIKA. I'm not trying to be funny Beti... Be careful.

SAIMA. Please don't be like this, I thought –

MALIKA. I wish your face lit up like that when you talked about my Azeem.

SAIMA. Well he doesn't make it easy, does he? My hope was, wishful thinking to be honest...

MALIKA. What?

SAIMA. That Azeem would come with me. Just for three days.

MALIKA. Azeem go with the Jamaat? It's not for him.

SAIMA. Don't be so sure Aunty, I've seen it first hand, the Jamaat has straightened more crooked characters than Azeem / believe you me.

MALIKA. He's your husband, have you forgotten that? Speak with respect.

(Silence.)

What's got you going like this?

SAIMA. Nothing.

MALIKA. Say it.

SAIMA. No, no Aunty, you rest, take care of your heart, make sure your health is okay.

MALIKA. Spit it out, you clearly want to.

SAIMA. Ask your handsome boy.

MALIKA. I'm asking *you.*

SAIMA. ...He drank Aunty. Okay. Alcohol. He's started drinking again.

(Pause.)

MALIKA. Is that why you want him to go on Jamaat with you?

SAIMA. That and, and for once actually show an interest in his faith, show an interest in what's important to me... and yes, people have gotten rid of stronger problems than alcohol with the Jamaat's help.

MALIKA. Don't call it a problem. It's a slip up, it – the stress of him being manager, new responsibilities, it must –

SAIMA. Not just about alcohol, it's about trust. This marriage. Me Aunty. <u>Me</u>.

(Silence.)

MALIKA. I'll have your uncle talk to Imran, bring the Jamaat to this home and Imran can explain things to Azeem. Invite him, in person, kindly, with love. Then, then you two can go on the ijtimah together.

SAIMA. You'll let the Jamaat come back into this home?

MALIKA. Azeem will see how important it is. How important it is for him to go. For him, for you, for his mother.

SAIMA. Azeem won't, he's not –

MALIKA. But meet me halfway Beti, okay?

SAIMA. What do you –

MALIKA. Don't go to the mosque tonight. Okay? Stay.

> *(Pause.)*

With your help he gave up drinking. With your support he's become a manager. He loves you, I know it. Yes, he made a mistake, but let's help him fix that mistake. A family comes together at times like this.

> *(Silence.)*

SAIMA. Aunty...

MALIKA. ...Yes Saima?

SAIMA. Come, lay back down, your eyebrows look terrible.

Scene Five

*(Later that night in the Bhatti living room.
The lights are off.* **SAIMA** *finishes lighting
small candles.* **AZEEM** *enters.)*

SAIMA. ...hey.

(Silence as **AZEEM** *takes in the view before
him. He turns the lights on.)*

AZEEM. This mean I'm off the sofa?

SAIMA. Don't – turn the lights back off.

AZEEM. Where's mum and dad?

SAIMA. Out.

AZEEM. Out where?

SAIMA. *Azeem.* Forget about your parents for a minute.

(Pause.)

AZEEM. I have a headache.

SAIMA. ...what's wrong?

AZEEM. Nothing.

SAIMA. You can talk to me.

AZEEM. Nothing to talk about.

SAIMA. Yes, there is.

(Silence.)

Why won't you open up / to me?

AZEEM. How was your meeting with Human Resources?

SAIMA. Answer –

AZEEM. What did Sheila say, or do you just save that topic
for Hamza?

SAIMA. ...I didn't speak to Sheila. I cancelled my appointment with H.R. I've made my decision. I don't want a transfer. I need a break. I'm leaving my job.

(Pause.)

Azeem, listen to me. I'm *exhausted*. Mentally, emotionally, in every way. I'm tired of explaining and explaining myself, I'm done. For my sanity's sake, I need to rest.

(Silence.)

AZEEM. ...Saima, please. I need you.

SAIMA. I'm here, not going –

AZEEM. Just do whatever it takes to make it work there and keep that job.

SAIMA. ...Tell me why?

(Pause.)

You used to talk to me.

(Pause.)

Talk to me?

AZEEM. ...Talking...

SAIMA. You used to trust me. Now you just pack it in. You don't even laugh with me anymore... You used to say, "I'm with you in a way that I'm with nobody else. With you, I'm somebody I didn't think I could be." And you really liked that. You used to be that way. Be that way again? ... Please?

(Pause.)

I miss the old Azeem.

(Silence.)

Fine. It's okay. It really is. Don't say anything. You don't have to explain anything to anyone...you can just be silent, and I'll be silent with you. I love you Azeem, you will eventually have to believe that. And if one day, you choose to open up to me, decide to be with me in a way, in a way that you're with nobody else, I'll be here...

(Silence.)

AZEEM. ...It's, it's not, not just idiots at your office, it won't –

SAIMA. Who else is –

AZEEM. This is just the beginning. With your hijab, it's only just starting, and we, this marriage, we're not strong enough to go through –

SAIMA. Yes we are, why couldn't –

AZEEM. For God's sake Saima, why don't you get – my problem is not – fine, what other people think, say, is an issue, but my issue – but not just that, it's not *just* that. Much more than that. I, I can't help you. And you will need help. I can't, I can't protect you, I can't – how can I? I'm only – I can't protect you from a whole country, a culture, a fucking civilisation. How can we survive that? If I can't protect you, protect <u>us</u>...if I can't protect us, then what am I? I'll be a lesser man than I already am.

(Pause.)

They didn't give me the job Saima. I didn't get the manager's position.

(Silence.)

SAIMA. But you've been working as manager for...for weeks, I...

(Pause.)

Are you at your old job?

AZEEM. No.

SAIMA. No? ... Did, did Richard let you go?

AZEEM. I quit.

SAIMA. You...you quit, you...quit?

> *(Silence.)*

You, you walked out of this door, every day, dressed for work, where, where the hell have you been going Azeem?

AZEEM. Getting paid. Working...at, at another branch, short term contract kind of –

SAIMA. Liar.

AZEEM. I'm, I'm not –

SAIMA. Don't you dare deny it, don't you fucking dare you – drinking was bad enough and now...

> *(Pause.)*

When you quit...did you think of me? Think of us?

AZEEM. Of course Saima, course I did.

SAIMA. ...Selfish.

AZEEM. Don't say that. You know me, I –

SAIMA. No I, I don't know you or who –

AZEEM. For fuck's sake, why're you takin it –

SAIMA. Who are you?

AZEEM. I'm Azeem Bhatti! That's who I am.

> *(Silence.)*

SAIMA. Go back. You didn't get sacked. Say you made a mistake. A big mistake. Ask David, ask him to help you get your old job back, beg them if you have to –

AZEEM. They already...

SAIMA. Already?

AZEEM. Already offered my old job back.

SAIMA. Great.

AZEEM. But, but I would have to apologise to Richard, only then –

SAIMA. I don't see the problem?

AZEEM. I can't apologise to Richard.

SAIMA. ...You can't apologise to Richard?

AZEEM. No.

SAIMA. You can't...but you can make me go to work and take my hijab off, carry this family on my shoulders... but you can't apologise? That's how little I mean to you?

AZEEM. Why are you takin it like this, for fuck's sake I'm not down and out, I'll get back on my feet, then you can wear the whole fuckin burkha for all I care.

SAIMA. ...I knew you were selfish. I didn't know you were scum.

AZEEM. ...Well now you know.

>   (**SAIMA** *grabs her jacket, hijab and purse. As she exits the home.*)

Saima.

SAIMA. What?

>   (*Pause.*)

What Azeem?

AZEEM. I... Look, I'm...

SAIMA. You're what?

>   (*Silence as* **AZEEM** *turns his back on her.*)

...I pity you, I really do.

Scene Six

(Later that night, **SAIMA** *and* **HAMZA** *in the main prayer room of the mosque.)*

SAIMA. Sorry, I didn't interrupt did I?

HAMZA. No you're / fine.

SAIMA. I didn't know where else...

HAMZA. You okay?

(Pause.)

What happened?

SAIMA. He lied.

HAMZA. Drink?

SAIMA. More.

HAMZA. Always more with him – sorry, I know, he's your –

SAIMA. No, don't be sorry.

HAMZA. What happened to the loyalty?

SAIMA. Fuck him.

HAMZA. Damn Saima.

SAIMA. What?

HAMZA. Just, damn... Look...this happens between – you see, marriage, marriage is a sacred...what I'm saying is, Azeem, he's not *all* bad.

SAIMA. He's not?

HAMZA. He's, he's got some, I guess –

SAIMA. Didn't think you would stick up for him.

HAMZA. Yeah, well...gotta always make excuses for a brother in our faith.

SAIMA. Thought you would be happy?

HAMZA. Happy you had another domestic?

SAIMA. Happy that I'm here.

(Silence.)

HAMZA. Erm, so, yeah. I, need, need to, er, to lock up and –

SAIMA. So lock up.

HAMZA. Right. Maybe, I, I could give you a lift back to –

SAIMA. I brought the car.

HAMZA. Brilliant. That's fanatastic. 'Cause, 'cause you don't want to, want to end up takin the bus, tube, public transport – late night, this time, not good time for, I've always said public transport at night can be really –

SAIMA. Hamza.

HAMZA. Yeah?

SAIMA. Shut up.

> (**SAIMA** *kisses* **HAMZA**. **HAMZA** *kisses her back.*)

ACT III

Scene One

(Later that week. **IMRAN JAMEEL** *in the Bhatti living room with* **AKEEL, MALIKA** *and* **SAIMA**.*)*

IMRAN. You redecorated?

AKEEL. I guess, yes, we have done some –

MALIKA. Not for a while.

IMRAN. No?

MALIKA. No.

IMRAN. Been that long I guess. Subhan'Allah. Wonderful taste. I can tell it must have been sister Malika.

AKEEL. I, I picked some thing's as well Imran, like this –

IMRAN. Come off it Akeel, I let you paint the mosque front door once and you had us looking like a post box. It's why we all call you postman pat.

AKEEL. *(Awkward laugh.)* Yes, yes, no, nobody calls me that anymore so...

MALIKA. Imran, when you speak to Azeem...

IMRAN. Yes?

MALIKA. He doesn't...he hasn't agreed to anything.

IMRAN. Oh, I, er, I see. Please, before you leave, call him, so I may speak –

MALIKA. Leave?

IMRAN. Sister Malika. I know it has been some time, but things remain the same, it is not, not right for the men and women to be in the same room. Even now, being so direct with you, I make an exception since we have known –

AKEEL. Of course that's, that's understandable, we were already –

MALIKA. This is my house. Me and Saima are not going anywhere.

IMRAN. ...I was invited here, asked to come. If I am, *if*, I am to give dawah to Azeem, then please, try to understand –

> *(Knock on the front door interrupts* **IMRAN.** **AKEEL** *opens the door and* **HAMZA** *enters.)*

HAMZA. Asalaam Alaikum Uncle.

AKEEL. Wa Alaikum Salaam son, I didn't realise –

IMRAN. Once Hamza realised I was returning to the Bhatti home, he insisted on coming, he was very excited to have Azeem come on Jamaat with us...son, you park the car okay?

HAMZA. Yeah, of course Dad, you could've parked a jumbo jet in that space.

IMRAN. He likes to tease me about my driving skills.

HAMZA. Or lack of them.

IMRAN. Okay, okay –

HAMZA. Where are my manners, asalaam alaikum Aunty.

MALIKA. Wa alaikum salaam Beta, how are you?

HAMZA. Alhamdulillah. *(To* **SAIMA.***)* Asalaam alaikum.

SAIMA. Salaam.

IMRAN. Like I was saying Sister Malika, women and men are usually separate, just like when we used to come –

HAMZA. Dad, I'm sure we can make an exception given the circumstances?

IMRAN. The laws of God can't be changed according to circumstances.

HAMZA. C'mon, I thought you wanted Azeem to come with the Jamaat? He sees we've sent his wife and mother out the room, what will he think? Just this once.

IMRAN. ...I guess, as long as it stays between us and word does not go out about it to others, this once, we, er, we could –

HAMZA. There we go! He's really a / softie at heart.

(*AZEEM enters.*)

IMRAN. Asalaam Alaikum Azeem Beta!

AZEEM. ...What's er, what's going on?

IMRAN. How are you son?

AZEEM. Wa Alaikum Salaam Uncle – Mum, what's, what's this?

MALIKA. It's okay.

AZEEM. No Mum it's – you don't have to put up with –

MALIKA. I invited them.

AZEEM. ...You invited...

(*Pause.*)

HAMZA. Mate, we're here to help you. To take you –

AZEEM. Help? You think I need help from a tosser / like you?

AKEEL. Azeem, they are guests in our home, speak respectfully.

IMRAN. ...Oh stop it Akeel, I've heard much worse come out of your mouth, he's a young man, full of life, we love the enthusiasm of youth in the Jamaat...see, son, I think you've misunderstood what the Jamaat is, perhaps... perhaps through your father, you haven't been able to see what the Tablighi Jamaat really is...come with us, find out for yourself, we all must take time away from worldly pursuits, get away from the distractions of the dunya, do some –

AZEEM. Uncle, stop. I'm not going anywhere. I don't care what anyone's told you, you're not welcome in this home.

HAMZA. Be respectful when you speak to your elders.

AZEEM. Shut up you little twat before I give you / a slap.

MALIKA. Azeem! Stop it. I want you to listen to Imran, he's / come here for you.

AZEEM. I don't have to listen / to anything.

IMRAN. Please, please Azeem, my boy, please, we came here only for one reason, there's an ijtimah taking place in Leeds soon, we invite you to join us for that. Three days. That's all. Come with us, please.

AZEEM. Uncle.

IMRAN. Yes?

AZEEM. Leeds is a shithole.

IMRAN. But you <u>must</u> come. Saima must have a male companion to accompany her.

(Pause.)

AZEEM. *(To* **SAIMA.***)* Tell me he's takin the piss?

(Pause.)

Don't, don't you think that was something you should've told me before –

SAIMA. Do you tell me everything Azeem?

MALIKA. Azeem, listen to me. No one is asking you to join the Jamaat. It's three days, it's nice to do something with your wife. The Jamaat helps people. Helps people break...old habits, and make new habits...understand?

IMRAN. Yes, yes, I once saw you pray at our mosque, many years ago, and I believe, if I remember correctly, you were praying with your elbows sticking out. Bad habit. We can help you with that, teach you how –

AZEEM. Elbows? Wow. May God forgive me. But tell me this Uncle, what will the Muslim community do if Mick Jagger became Muslim?

IMRAN. Who is this Mick –

AZEEM. What would you do with his elbows?

HAMZA. Ignore him Dad, he's being stupid.

AZEEM. Stupid? If it can happen to Cat Stevens why not Jagger?

IMRAN. ...I don't wish to be stark, but Azeem, you must understand, coming with the Jamaat is something every Muslim should do.

AZEEM. Uncle, there's more than one way to be a Muslim. You see, truth is, you lot are the reason us Muslims are weak in this country. Ever since you got off the boat, *you and your village Islam lot have done nothing to create a space for us in this society, nothing to make us powerful in this...so you see why there will be no space for you in this home. Please see your way out.

MALIKA. *Okay, that's enough now.

AKEEL. *Azeem, bas.

IMRAN. ...I see. I... I didn't know you felt this strong... seems like this has been a wasted trip.

(Pause.)

Thank you for your time and welcoming us back into this home. Come Hamza...asalaam alaikum.

(IMRAN *approaches the main door,* HAMZA *does not move.*)

Hamza...come.

HAMZA. One minute Dad. I want to give this one more shot.

AZEEM. Don't waste your time mate.

HAMZA. You don't like Leeds.

AZEEM. No.

HAMZA. That's okay. Leeds isn't the only place the Jamaat goes.

AZEEM. I'm not going to India.

HAMZA. Oh no, I'm referring to places much closer, say, a place like Woking. Woking is pretty. You like Woking Azeem?

AZEEM. ...I've never been.

HAMZA. You've never been?

AZEEM. No.

HAMZA. Right.

IMRAN. Enough now Hamza / let's leave.

HAMZA. One sec Dad...that is a shame. I had suggested Woking to Saima as a day trip, for you two to take.

MALIKA. Why's that? Why a trip to Woking?

HAMZA. Let's ask Azeem Aunty. Azeem, why do you think Woking?

(*Pause.*)

...Answer's obvious... Shah Jahan Mosque obviously. The first mosque built in Britain. You surely knew about that didn't you Azeem?

AZEEM. No afraid not.

IMRAN. *Hamza.* Not another word. We are leaving.

HAMZA. ...As you wish Dad.

(**HAMZA** *joins* **IMRAN** *by the exit.*)

IMRAN. *(To* **AKEEL** *and* **MALIKA**). Don't mind him, you see, Hamza gets excited about Woking because it's been like a second home for us. We have so much family there, my siblings live there, so, you see my nephews, Hamza's cousins, they have three shops, owned for many –

AZEEM. Ha! You lot have a cornershop as well, typical.

HAMZA. What was that?

AZEEM. Nothing.

HAMZA. Oh, it was something. Are we too backward for you? First the "village Islam," now a "cornershop"?

AZEEM. No. Just a joke.

HAMZA. A joke? Hmm. That makes sense. After all, you are a funny guy Azeem. Always with the jokes. You know what? If you really wanted to do something to earn some fast cash you could've just done a bit of stand up comedy. Plenty of comedy clubs in Woking. Why, instead, you chose to work as a <u>waiter</u>, at a Pakistani restaurant, is beyond me. Wearing a bow tie, dancing to the tune of drunk white people, and yet, *we* are the backward ones?

SAIMA. Did you say waiter, Azeem works as a waiter? At a restaurant?

HAMZA. Yeah, that's right.

AZEEM. He's talking shit.

HAMZA. Saw you Azeem, with my own eyes, when I went to visit my cousin.

MALIKA. You must have seen / somebody else.

AKEEL. My son is a manager.

HAMZA. I don't think he –

AZEEM. Why don't you fuck off out of here now, come round my house preaching to me, go on. *(Pushes* **HAMZA***.)* Fuck off out of here!

    *(*MALIKA *stops* AZEEM*.)*

MALIKA. Not in this house Azeem, don't you dare raise your hand.

IMRAN. This is not right. I won't tolerate my son being treated like this. We came to your home for you and then you treat us like –

MALIKA. I think we should all calm down and take a moment –

AKEEL. I won't tolerate false rumors about my son Imran. How do you expect him –

IMRAN. Let's go Hamza. We should never have come –

HAMZA. Uncle, they're not false –

AKEEL. Yes they are!

IMRAN. My son does not lie.

AKEEL. My son got *promoted* to a manager's position. He's been working there for weeks. It might be hard for you to believe that he achieved something that you and me – achieved something our generation couldn't, something even your own son couldn't, that, that gives you no right to come into my home and lie like –

AZEEM. Forget them Dad, don't waste – let them go. Leave it.

AKEEL. No one goes anywhere. This is not a joke, I won't have false rumors spread about my son, make a shame of our name in the community, over some, have people talk – now Hamza, you think real hard on what I'm about to ask you...what did you really see in Woking?

(Pause.)

HAMZA. ...Uncle... Uncle I –

IMRAN. Brother Akeel... Hamza is telling the truth. I have also seen Azeem at the restaurant. I went to visit my brother a few days back and I saw. I didn't bring it up because I know it can be embarrassing, you pride yourself on being a family of educated professionals. But don't ask Hamza. Ask me. You've known me over thirty years, I'm telling you, I saw him.

(Pause.)

AKEEL. You are a liar as well. You defend your son.

IMRAN. Akeel, let's not say things that cannot –

AKEEL. Get out of my house. You will do anything to get one over me won't you? To, to elevate yourself over me in this community, make me look bad, fine. But not my son.

IMRAN. See sense Akeel, this is me. Imran.

SAIMA. Uncle. You're making a mistake.

MALIKA. Saima?

SAIMA. Uncle Imran is not lying.

AZEEM. Don't do this now, not in front of –

SAIMA. Azeem never got the manager's job, he lied. To all of us. To me.

MALIKA. Saima, let's not, some things are not to be talked about in front of others, just, just be quiet and later, later we will –

SAIMA. Sorry Aunty, but I won't be silent.

IMRAN. ...I think now me and Hamza are both owed an apology.

AKEEL. ...Are you deaf Imran? I said get out.

IMRAN. ...Fine. Have it your way. Come, Hamza, let's go.

HAMZA. But Dad, Saima still wants to go to / Leeds.

SAIMA. Don't talk for me Hamza. You heard your dad. Go. Leave.

IMRAN. I tell you, gratitude is a lost virtue...may God have mercy on the Bhatti family...asalaam alaikum.

     (**IMRAN** *and* **HAMZA** *exit.*)

AZEEM. ...I... I wanted to tell you –

MALIKA. *(To* **SAIMA.***)* How dare you.

SAIMA. What?

MALIKA. How dare you humiliate my son, this family like that?

AZEEM. Mum, leave it.

SAIMA. Your son has been lying to you, to his wife, all of us and you're mad at me, I'm in the wrong?

MALIKA. Yes. His is a mistake. What you did, that is no mistake. You're at fault here.

SAIMA. I'm at fau – no. I'm not taking it. You can't do this again.

MALIKA. Again?

     (Pause.)

What again?

SAIMA. This is what you did to your daughter, to Javeria, always blamed her, made her at fault, I won't suffer like her. No. I refuse to end up like that.

AZEEM. Don't say that to – Dad, please, can you take Mum upstairs.

MALIKA. Acha, showing your true colours now aren't you Saima?

AZEEM. Mum, please, can you leave me alone with my wife?

AKEEL. Come Malika, your son is asking.

MALIKA. I always knew it, you don't know what it means to be a wife, no, you don't have it in you. Someone like you can never be part of this family. You don't know loyalty. You don't know real love. You only care about –

AZEEM. *Enough.* No more. Alright? Enough.

AKEEL. Challo. Bas. Kafi ho gaya.

(**AKEEL** *exits with* **MALIKA.**)

AZEEM. I think, she's...she just doesn't know how to handle the... I should've told her the truth, I, I should've just –

SAIMA. Why didn't you tell me you were working as a waiter? Why didn't you ever say to me, "I never got the promotion Saima." Why...why weren't you truthful with me?

AZEEM. I was hoping.

SAIMA. For what?

AZEEM. For, for it all to work out, for me to make it right, for me to show...show you the man you married Saima, who he really is, what he's made of...

(*Pause.*)

SAIMA. ...When uncle hit aunty, what did you do?

AZEEM. What do you –

SAIMA. Do you remember what you did?

AZEEM. No.

SAIMA. You did nothing. You froze Azeem. And I saw in your face, a scared boy. And I thought I could help you. But I can't. I can't carry your pain.

AZEEM. What, what're you saying?

SAIMA. I'm... I'm leaving you.

>   *(Pause.)*

AZEEM. ...Don't.

SAIMA. I have to.

AZEEM. You don't have –

SAIMA. Yes I do. You don't understand, there's no...

AZEEM. What?

SAIMA. ...I owe you the truth.

>   *(Pause.)*

Last week, after you told me... I went to Hamza. I made a mistake. I, I kissed him.

>   *(Small pause, then **AZEEM** laughs.)*

AZEEM. Bullshit, why're you saying this?

SAIMA. It was wrong. And I'm sorry.

AZEEM. ...You didn't, you, you would never do –

SAIMA. I wouldn't. And I don't want turn into that, someone, someone I hate, see, Azeem, you go down and you take me down with you. But I won't let that happen to me. You're...you're not good for me.

>   *(**SAIMA** takes her wedding ring off and puts it down.)*

I deserve better.

Scene Two

*(A few days later, still in the living room of
the Bhatti home with* **JAVERIA** *and* **AZEEM**.)

JAVERIA. ...Can't believe it...you finally did it. You finally pushed her over the edge.

AZEEM. Thanks big sister.

JAVERIA. You've actually proved my theory that no woman can live with you.

AZEEM. Are you here to help me feel better?

JAVERIA. I am. I brought you biryani. Feel better?

AZEEM. Twat.

JAVERIA. I'm sorry, I'll stop, I promise.

AZEEM. How was Saima?

JAVERIA. Okay.

AZEEM. Did she, she ask, or say anything about...

*(***JAVERIA*** shakes her head to say "no.")*

JAVERIA. You'll have to let it go... I'm here now. Okay? You're not on your own, with mum and dad, I'm going to come visit more often. Have them round to my house as well, so you can have your own time. We'll be okay. You'll be –

AZEEM. You mean that?

JAVERIA. I promise, it'll be –

AZEEM. No, not that. You're here now? Mum and dad will have you?

JAVERIA. ...Insha'Allah, yes.

AZEEM. ...Okay...

(Pause.)

JAVERIA. What?

    (Pause.)

Azeem?

AZEEM. I'm leaving.

JAVERIA. ...When are you coming back?

AZEEM. I'm not.

JAVERIA. Are you, you're not thinking –

AZEEM. I'm packed. Stuff is in the car. I'm off.

JAVERIA. When?

AZEEM. Now.

JAVERIA. *Now?* You are insane. Where, where're you going?

AZEEM. I'm gonna spend a week at a friend's, then, I'm going to book a flight, and I'm going to leave.

JAVERIA. Where?

AZEEM. I don't know yet.

JAVERIA. Oh my god, a man with plan huh?

AZEEM. Baji... I can't stay here, not in this home, not here. That's all I know. There's nothing to stay for.

    (Pause.)

Please Baji, listen to me? You, you had your escape. You left. You figured it out and I stayed and carried it on my shoulders. Can I...isn't it right that I have my turn now? Where's my chance?

JAVERIA. ...I am listening to you Azeem, but, I'll be here, but please be here with me, going away, starting again, that's not the solution for you –

AZEEM. Then what is?

JAVERIA. You... I, I don't know.

AZEEM. Then let me go and find out for myself.

(Pause.)

I'm begging you, please Baji, let me go?

(Silence.)

JAVERIA. Go somewhere with a lot of brown people.

AZEEM. You mean like Pakistan?

JAVERIA. I was thinking more like Bradford.

(They laugh.)

AZEEM. ...No. Forget that. Nowhere in Britain. Fuck this country.

JAVERIA. Pakistan it is then?

AZEEM. Fuck that country as well.

JAVERIA. ...There's no, no way you'll change your mind?

AZEEM. Why?

JAVERIA. Because *I'll miss you* befkoof.

*(**MALIKA** enters.)*

MALIKA. Beti, we're getting late.

JAVERIA. Sure Mum, just one – let's finish this after mum's appointment?

AZEEM. It's already finished.

MALIKA. What are you talking about?

(Pause.)

What?

AZEEM. Mum, I... I'm –

JAVERIA. Azeem's going to a friend's, for a little while.

MALIKA. Which friend? Who? It's not a good idea. Stay here.

JAVERIA. It'll be good for him to clear his head. I'm staying for a little while Mum.

MALIKA. You're staying?

JAVERIA. Yeah. Let Azeem go.

MALIKA. ...I don't like it.

AZEEM. Mum... I'm going.

MALIKA. Nobody listens to me anymore.

AZEEM. You know that's not true.

MALIKA. We'll talk about this later. Come Beti, we're getting late.

JAVERIA. Mein dho tyaar hoon.

MALIKA. Azeem...have you eaten?

AZEEM. Ate something –

MALIKA. Make sure you eat, okay?

AZEEM. Yeah –

MALIKA. Promise?

AZEEM. Promise...see, I do still listen to you.

MALIKA. Stupid boy.

MALIKA.	JAVERIA.
Salaam Beta.	Salaam.

> (**MALIKA** *exits followed by* **JAVERIA.** *A few moments later* **JAVERIA** *runs back in and hugs* **AZEEM** *tightly. She smacks him on the head and leaves.* **AKEEL** *enters.*)

AKEEL. They gone?

AZEEM. Just left.

AKEEL. ...You heard from Saima?

AZEEM. No.

(Silence.)

I'm er, leaving for a bit.

AKEEL. Leaving?

AZEEM. Stay with a friend. Short while.

AKEEL. ...Why are you telling me? I don't care. Your life. Do what you wish.

> (**AZEEM** *puts on his jacket and takes his car keys.*)

You should have treated her better.

AZEEM. *(Laughs.)* Okay.

AKEEL. Why are you laughing?

AZEEM. Nothing.

AKEEL. I'm not a clown. Why are you laughing?

AZEEM. I'll stop.

AKEEL. I know, I know – you er, you blame me, don't you? Don't you? You, you think somehow, somehow this is down –

AZEEM. Didn't say –

AKEEL. I did right by you, I did better than most, a roof over your head, food in your stomach, not once did you go –

AZEEM. You think maybe there's more to being a father than a roof and food.

AKEEL. See! I knew it, salaa, I knew it, that's what you think. No, not my fault. I did right by everyone, this is all your fault.

AZEEM. Not my fault, don't say that.

AKEEL. Don't try and, and, you're at fault. Yes you and only you! I was a good father, I set a good example, I / was a good –

AZEEM. A good – what kind of father hits his son? What kind of father beats their mother in front of his children? What kind...

(*Pause.*)

You were supposed to protect me.

(*Silence.*)

I'm leaving.

AKEEL. ...you said.

AZEEM. Leaving for good. Not coming back.

AKEEL. ...For, for good?

AZEEM. Yes. I'm going to –

AKEEL. Good! Leave. Go. Get lost. We don't want you here anyway.

AZEEM. ...Alright. If that's the way you want it.

(*Pause.*)

I am sorry Dad.

AKEEL. (*As* **AZEEM** *exits.*) Don't be...

(**AZEEM** *halts.*)

...Don't be sorry... I... I didn't do... I didn't show you what a good husband is.

AZEEM. Don't be too hard on yourself old man.

AKEEL. I'm not old, I grew up on buffalo milk.

AZEEM. Yeah, course, forgot about that.

(*Pause.*)

Can, can I ask you something?

AKEEL. Ask me something?

AZEEM. Yeah.

AKEEL. ...ask.

AZEEM. ...say, er, say we hadn't moved here from Pakistan. We were born there. Grew up there. In your village, living next door to family, the whole big, extended family stuff. Surrounded by cousins, aunties, uncles. All taking care of each other, looking out for each other. On our own land, that we had owned for centuries and made our money –

AKEEL. But we didn't own that land for centuries. That land was given to us in Partition. The little land we owned in Pakistan, that, that we only had for a few decades. Our real land, which we had owned for centuries, was in India, given away to someone else.

AZEEM. Okay, so, so say you were in your land, in India, and stayed there instead –

AKEEL. Why would I be in India? My land is Pakistan.

AZEEM. Okay – God, no wonder we're a mess. So you're –

AKEEL. What are you trying ask? Say it?

AZEEM. I'm, I'm trying to ask, where is my land? Where do I call home?

AKEEL. Here. Britain. Thought you would call this home. What else did I make those sacrifices for? Thought, you would make it in this country, this land would –

AZEEM. Make it, in this land? Dad, we've been trying. You have. I have. And we're worse off than before.

(Pause.)

We've lost Dad. There's nothing for us here.

AKEEL. I, I don't know what you want from – I tried my best. I did all –

AZEEM. I know, I'm not, you did your best... I know.

AKEEL. ...Where, where are you going?

AZEEM. I don't know. All I know is it can't be here. I can't stay in this country.

AKEEL. You sound like me. I said the same thing. But, but for you, it, it should've been different...then what was it all for? The sacrifices. The hate. The hardship. We could have just stayed in Pakistan...at least there, there was sunshine.

AZEEM. Look, I'll find somewhere, then I'll let you –

AKEEL. Go somewhere where there's sunshine.

AZEEM. Sure. Why not. I'll send you a postcard.

AKEEL. You can friend me on Facebook. I have Facebook now.

AZEEM. Just as well I'm leaving the country.

AKEEL. ...I'm not surprised though. No. Not surprised you didn't get promoted. They don't like promoting Pakistanis here, I know it.

AZEEM. Now that you mention it. I, er, actually had this informal type of meeting, with the Clapham folk, at the Ritz...

AKEEL. Okay?

AZEEM. And I got dressed up. But, er, but I didn't wear a tie.

AKEEL. You didn't wear – see! That's why you / didn't get the manager's position.

AZEEM. Didn't get the manager's position. Exactly.

(*Pause.*)

AKEEL. Your grandfather always wore a tie. He was a respected man. We all were, once. Once...once we were all respected.

(**AKEEL** *approaches* **AZEEM.** **AKEEL,** *with his hands raised, recites Surah Ad Duha in Arabic for* **AZEEM.**)

وَالضُّحَىٰ

وَاللَّيْلِ إِذَا سَجَىٰ

مَا وَدَّعَكَ رَبُّكَ وَمَا قَلَىٰ

وَلَلْآخِرَةُ خَيْرٌ لَكَ مِنَ الْأُولَىٰ

By the morning, bright,
and the night, when it is calm,
your Lord has not left you,
and is not incensed:
and the future will be better for you than the past;
Ya'Allah, let his future be better than the past
Allah, let his future be better than the past
let his future be better than the past.

(*As* **AKEEL** *nears the end of the recitation,* **AZEEM** *breaks down and drops his head on his father's shoulder.* **AKEEL** *awkwardly embraces his son and comforts him.* **AZEEM** *regains his composure and reins in his tears.*)

...Ameen.

(*To transfer the blessing of the recitation,* **AKEEL** *blows on* **AZEEM**'s *face and rubs his head, face and chest with the palms of his hands.*)

AZEEM. Yeah, thanks for the germs.

AKEEL. Go on...get lost. Go. Get out of here. Don't ever show your face here again.

(**AKEEL** *exits. As he leaves,* **AZEEM** *takes in one last look of the Bhatti home. As he closes the front door, he gazes though the windows of the living room onto the streets of modern day Britain.* **AZEEM** *disappears.*)

End of Play

GLOSSARY

Alhamdulillah: (Al-hamdu lil lah) is an Arabic phrase meaning "thanks be to God." It is often used in everyday life by Muslims to express gratitude to God.

Asalaam Alaikum: (As-Salaam-Alaikum) Arabic for "peace be with you," a common Muslim greeting.

Asr: Is the late afternoon prayer and the third of the five daily prayers in Islam.

Astaghfirullah: (As tagh fir ul lah) An Arabic word that means "I seek forgiveness from God."

Ayat ul Kursi: The name means "the verse of the Throne." It is ayah/verse 225 from Surah/Chapter 2 of the Qur'an. The Surah/Chapter is titled Al-Baqara (The Cow). An important verse in Islamic belief, the recitation of which is said to bring many benefits, one of which is protection or safety from harm.

Baqwas: Punjabi colloquialism meaning "rubbish" or "nonsense."

Chilla: Persian and Arabic that literally translates to mean "forty." Often used to denote forty days and nights of solitude or spiritual retreat of some kind.

Dawa: (Da'wah) Arabic for "invitation," used to "invite" people to Islam.

Dunya: Originally an Arabic word that has been incorporated into many other languages. It means the temporal, earthly world.

Eid: Arabic for festival or holiday. It refers to the two religious holidays that take place annually, Eid al-Fitr (Feast of Breaking the Fast) and Eid al-Adha (Feast of the Sacrifice).

Fazail-e-Amaal: The principal text of the Tablighi Jamaat.

Friday prayer: Also known as the Jumu'ah prayer, it is prayed every Friday at the mosque in congregation after a sermon. It replaces the midday prayer, Zuhr.

Gora: Hindi/Urdu term, means "fair," used to refer to someone who is fair skinned or white/Caucasian.

Halal: An Arabic term, means "religiously permissible." When used in reference to food, it denotes foods that are considered permissible for Muslims to eat. The alternate category would be haram or something that is "religiously impermissible," such as pork.

Heer: From the Punjabi love story of *Heer Ranjha*. In this story Heer was known as an extremely beautiful woman and is used here as term of endearment.

Insha'Allah: (in sha-Allah) Arabic for "God willing."

Ijtimah: Urdu for "gathering."

Ittar: Natural perfume that is alcohol free.

Janazah prayer: The Islamic funeral prayer performed as part of the funeral ritual.

Maghrib: Is the evening prayer, prayed just after sunset and the fourth of the five daily prayers.

Sajda: When one is in prostration.

Subhan'Allah: Arabic for "Glory be to God."

Sufi: A follower of Sufism. Sufism, known as Tasawwuf amongst Muslims, is an aspect of Islam that highlights the mystical and spiritual dimension of the Islamic religion.

Tablighi Jamaat: (Tab-lee-gee Ja-maat) A religious revivalist movement, started in India in 1927 by Muhammad Ilyas al-Kandhlawi.

Ummah: An Arabic word that means "nation'" or "community." It denotes here the global Muslim community.

Ummah'ti Muhammad: The community of Muhammad (peace and blessings be upon him.)

Zuhr: Is the midday prayer and the second of the five daily prayers. On Friday's the Zuhr prayer is replaced by the Jumu'ah prayer (Friday prayer).

CPSIA information can be obtained
at www.ICGtesting.com
Printed in the USA
LVHW012004151221
706295LV00017B/2307

9 780573 709418